冯汉骥全集 ⑥

人类学卷

冯汉骥 著　张勋燎 白 彬 主编

巴蜀书社

论文集

彝族的历史起源

彝族为中国西南重要的少数民族。他们在其居住之地区世代相传，名称多变，距今已近两千年。其现在之人数不详，有学者估计总数约三百万。[①] 四川之彝族估计约有一百万，居住在一万一千平方英里的土地之上。看来上述人数估计均偏高，其总数可能仅一百万左右。

彝族散居于云南山区及四川西南部。其分布西延至湄公河谷，在历史上东边曾达贵州西部。越南北部边境地区亦有小群彝族居住。

---

① 此数为 Terrien de Lacouperie 所估计，见 The Language of China before the Chinese，Trans. *Philological Soc.*，1885–86，P.479，Frederick Stan 引此数字，见 Lolo objects in the Public Museum Miluaukee，*Bull*，1911，Vol. I，Pt.2，PP.209 ~ 20. E.PITTARD，in *Les races et l'histoire*，1924，P.495，又引用 Stan 所使用之资料。杨成志在《罗罗说略》中重述 pittard 之所引，见《岭南学报》第一卷第三期，第 134 ~ 152 页。尽管此数目出现在最近的论文中，却只不过是 Lacouperie 之猜测而已。《科学》杂志编者在 1934 年第 18 卷、第 1672 页中估计，四川境内之彝族大致一百万；然此数仅据 W.R Morse, The Nosu Tribes of Western Szechuan, Chin.med.Jour.，March，1933.这些数字均非出自计算，言过其实。"中国西部科学院"之调查表明，四川之黑彝不足二十万，白彝未逾八十万，见《特刊》1935 年第 1 卷。此数可信。调查者在凉山地区实地计算了彝族家庭成员。

在东北方，彝族沿着与东北向流之金沙江平行的大凉山向北深入，直达大渡河以南之嘉定、雅州。此一狭长地带约150英里长，不到100英里宽。山地崎岖，乃彝族独立生存之乡。其西部有藏、西番和麽些诸部落。北邻西番，东南方则有分散的掸、苗部落。

彝族居住之地区，乃西藏高原之东南边缘。长江上游及其支流横贯其间。水流湍急，不能航行。气候温和，然冬季酷冷。

彝族聚居之地理位置，不仅对其本身重要，且扼亚洲东南各族移徙之关隘。彝族虽有文字，[1]但就目前所知，并无历史文献。现在有关其历史之原始资料，仅有内容贫乏而经常记载不确的汉文史书。

"罗罗"之称，始于元朝，亦即此名称，已有八百年之历史。人们以为"罗罗"乃卢鹿；卢鹿者，公元五至九世纪东爨土著部落之名也[2]。"罗罗"是否即卢鹿，实难判定。然元朝确在建川河谷之北，设有行政区罗罗斯宣慰司[3]。

今彝族各部落对自己之称呼，相异颇大；词首之辅音极少用"L"，元音又各不一致；第二音节通常用"so"或"su"，有时又略

---

[1]　彝文乃一种象形文字，略仿汉字。汉文资料指出，此种彝文为名叫阿比之彝人在公元550年所创。彝文之创造，彝族中传说有三。阿比称其所创文字为"文书"，即标准文字也；汉族称之为舞文。彝文主要用于宗教文件，惟"毕摩"（"白马"）能读释。然毕摩仅能读懂自己部族之文字。丁文江在《漫游散记》中对此有述，见《独立评论》1933年第35卷第13页，及第42卷第19—20页，D'OLLONE 在 In Forbidden China 第106—107页，亦有所述。今已有涉及彝文之大量文献。丁文江做了全新及广泛的工作，见1936年《爨文丛刊》；亦见杨成志《罗罗之字体和文书》，1935年。

[2]　《炎徼纪闻》4：17a，"罗罗本卢鹿而讹"。亦见 PELLIOT, Deux itineeraires de Chine en Inde，（《从印度到中国之两次行》）BEFEO 4（1904），137。

[3]　参见《新元史》卷二四八。

去第二音节。①外国调查者对彝族之称谓，变化多端，其理论并无多大助益。②

"罗罗"一词系八百年前之汉语音译。译时或许即欠准确，亦或该词乃地方方言。可能数百年来，汉语、彝语之语音均有变化。以我等现今之知识，欲定其名称之起源及含义，必将造成错误，因其中未知之因素过多。我们当前所能判断者，仅知此词非始于外国，但其语源则不详。

"罗罗"一词虽元朝即已产生，然直至明朝，方始广泛采用。《南诏野史》记载了臣属于南诏掸国之十一个彝族部落③。此等部落之名称，并非由于其种族之不同，大部分系因特殊之文化，如衣着、职业、风俗之不同而异。有时，即简单地采用了统治家族之名称。随着

---

① 此中一些差异是：Mo-su，Mou-su，Ngo-gu，Ne-su，Nei-su，No-Su，No，Na，以及Lei-su。在四川，他们被称之为"蛮子"，或"蛮家"，后者为较礼貌之称呼。在滇南，掸族称其为"蒙"。

② Lacouperie，op.cit.，pp.480-81称"罗罗"源于"卢鹿"，而"卢鹿"又源于"罗鬼"（Lo-Kuei）。"罗鬼"之说实误，乃贬义绰号，此为近称，即非"罗罗"，又非"卢鹿"。

Paul Vial 在 "Les Lolos"（《罗罗各部》1898）中解释，汉族以其音悦而重译此音。此亦非也。较早之汉文书籍将其写为卢鹿人，后又缩写之，倘此名为卢应写为卢人。

Lietard 认为"Lolo"系"No-so"之误，"No-so"为"罗罗"人自称，见（Au Yunnan，Les Lo-lo P，o，1913）。 然 Shirokogoroff 在 Phoneetic Notes on a Lolo Dialect and the Co sonant L，（Academia Sinica，Bull.，Vol.1，No.2，P.183）中认为，音节"No"与"so"，其义在彝族中极为不同，任何语源学的派生均不可靠；此使 Litard 之解释失去意义。Shirokogoroff 乃作出若干假设，谓"罗罗"或许有政治原因，如"满州"之称，或则邻居对其特定称呼，如通古斯之称；亦或从古迹中抄录者。

S.C.Clarke 在 Among the tribes of Southwest China 文中从传教士 C.C.Hicks 之说（The Nou Su，Chinese Recorder，41，PP.21ff），即"罗罗"之名为彝族祭祀祖先所用竹制小箩箩得名。Clarke 谓，汉族据此诨称之。此极不可信。

C.E Jamieson The Aborigines of western China（China Journal of Art and Science1，pp.376ff.） 引用十九世纪中国作者张寅之说，即"罗罗"为"科罗"（kolo）类人猿之后裔，"科罗"衍变"罗罗"。此全然与历史事实不符。

③ 《南诏野史》卷二。Lietard（前引）称，此大多数名称为汉族虚构。此为矛盾之说。他本人列数二十以上之部落名称，其中大多数与《南诏野史》所列相同。

部落迁徙，家族灭绝，某一名称亦随之消失，但这并非意味着一个部族集团之消失。在独立之彝族部落中，据说有黑彝二十六部，白彝三十部，混合部落三个，奴隶部落两个。[①] 早期之汉文书籍，亦有相同之记载。

在中国西南各族中，广泛流行黑、白之称，但其涵义则各不相同。有时，此称呼代表服装之颜色，如黑苗、白苗即是一例，[②] 在湘南，某一部族之被称之黑苗，则因其开化程度不如靠近汉族之苗人，[③] 生息在湄公河上游、与彝族缘近之傈僳族，其黑傈僳、白傈僳之称，亦同出一因。[④] 通常这些民族自己并不如此称呼，以黑、白区分之者乃汉族。

然而彝族却与此不同，他们自己划分成黑白两部。一些西方观察者完全混淆这种区别[⑤]。在云南，黑彝由统治家族构成；所有居其下者，皆为白彝。在四川，黑彝则居多数。

彝族中黑彝、白彝之分，早已有之。《蛮书》《新唐书》即有黑

---

① Lietard，前引。其资料为第二手，且未进一步解释。d'Ollone 于 1908–1909 年遍访彝区，谓各部族占据之地域相互妥订，侵犯了令人忿恨，故而行中不得不经常更换向导。

② Clark, op.cit., p.371.

③ Jamieson, op.cit., pp.381—82.

④ A.Rose and J.C.Brown, "Li-su（Yawyin）Tribes of the Burma-China Frontier", *Memoirs*, *Asiatic Society of Bengal*, Vol.Ⅲ, 1910–14, pp.249–76.

⑤ Jamieson, op.cit., p.381. 他称：黑色一词源于皮肤之颜色。Buxton 在 *The peoptes of Asia* p.156 中重复此说。事实上，彝族之肤色较大多数土著居民为浅。许多观察家均有记载。一些观察家甚而称"罗罗"之肤色比南欧人还白皙。倘黑彝之称因肤色之故，则白彝以何谓之？Lietard 以为"Lolo"之名系从"No-so"演变而来，又因"诺"（*No*）含黑色之意，汉文按 Lolo 音译乃误。此假设前已提及。

蛮、白蛮之记载。[①]此种区分或许意味着种族之差异，至少确切地表明两者语言之不同。[②]

今之彝族中，黑彝、白彝体格有别。黑彝身材高大，有的报告谓其身材较欧洲人还高，鹰钩鼻、高鼻梁，总体观之，与蒙古人种显然有异。[③]白彝多似蒙古人种，体格较差，头部指数亦与黑彝略别。[④]

云南之黑彝构成统治阶级，四川之黑彝还统治了黔西之苗族。黑乃显贵之标志，黑彝只在其内部通婚。云南之黑彝时有将其女儿嫁给汉族官吏之子或高贵汉族世家。[⑤]而四川之黑彝则严格实行族内婚。

此种情况可能解释为：黑彝或许源于一个单独族系之征服集团，而白彝则是被征服之另一些种族集团，以后逐渐接受了征服者之语言。此过程在四川之彝族中仍在进行。在云南，黑彝或在战争中被汉族统治者杀戮，或向北退却。故而云南所谓之彝族之大多数，属于较低下之白彝；少数统治家族仍居原地，接受了汉族统治者所授官职。

尽管彝族在很早以前即为汉族所知，然在汉文资料中涉及彝族者极少。又因其它部族之存在，实情常被弄混。某些记载中之部落，要确定其是否为彝族，殊感困难。在本文的历史研究中，我们可以从

① 在《新唐书》卷二二二提到诸如乌蛮：东爨（罗罗）、哀牢、南诏、施蛮、顺蛮、裸蛮等，及白蛮：西爨、弄栋蛮、青蛉蛮。

② 《蛮书》卷八："言语音，白蛮最正，蒙舍蛮次之，诸部落不如也。"

③ 从马哥·波罗到今之旅行家，均记下其详细特征，E.C.Baber谓"他们较欧洲人高"，此似夸大之词。d'Ollone, op.cit., p.51, 称："彝人无亚洲人特点，非黄色皮肤，呈黝黑色，如南欧人之肤色，其目深而大，弓眉护之，鹰钩鼻，口正。"

④ Cf.A.Legender, "Far west Chinois", Tp, 1909, tab.A–C.Dixon, *Racial History of man*, p.281, 作了分析。亦见丁文江《漫游散记》。

⑤ 关于此一婚俗，见J K.Shryock, "Ch'en Ting's Account of the Marriage Customs of Chief of Yunnan and Kueichou", *Amer. Anthro. 36*, No.4, Oct.–Dec.1934.

黔西北水西①地区开始，此地为彝族头人安氏②大家族统治之地区。

在周朝，水西为牂牁、③且兰④所辖。约在公元前四世纪末，被楚将庄蹻所征服。而在公元前316年，与楚敌对之秦，派司马错占领其地。彼时此地居民之情况，我们一无所知。

西汉前期，水西属夜郎⑤国之域。时夜郎为中国西南最大、最强之国家。当代学者王静如从语言学角度论定夜郎居民乃彝族之祖先。⑥此说可得到历史依据之印证。

东汉后期，此地区据说为水西彝族安氏家族之祖先所统治。《读史方舆纪要》对水西安氏家族有如下记载：

水西宣慰司⑦在贵阳府西北三百里。土酋安氏，世守其地。其先济火⑧之后也。蜀汉建兴三年（公元226年），诸葛武侯南征，牂牁帅济火积粮，通道以迎。武侯表封罗甸国王。⑨居普里，即今普定卫。⑩

---

① 水西，今大定、黔西附近。水西之名，始于明朝。其界域时有变化。

② 安氏家庭自称其祖先乃公元第三世纪之济火，然在明朝之前安氏之名不见使用。

③ 一说牂牁者，系船之桩也，庄蹻远征时人们设想其船队停靠于此地，故名。然郑珍谓，在庄蹻远征之很久以前，牂牁之名即有之，见《巢经巢文集·牂牁考》。此地之宽度不明。

④ 且兰，一小国，汉武帝并之，其地今贵州之平越。

⑤ *Han shu*, Tung-wen ed., ch.95.p.1 "南夷君长以十数，夜郎最大。"

⑥ 王静如："A Comparative Linguistic study on the Songs of Bair-Long Tribe", *Acdademia sinica Nat. Res.Inst.of History and philology*, mon.8, Hsi-hsia yen-chiu, pp.15-54.

⑦ 水西宣慰司，明朝首建。

⑧ 济火，《明史》称火济。

⑨ 罗甸在东汉之后靠近牂牁地区。罗甸一词可能与"罗罗"有些联系，因"甸"有领地或国家之意。

⑩ 普定卫，在安顺县北约22.5公里处。在宋朝，此处称为普里蛮部。元时，此地称普定路，云南辖属。明朝，更名为今安顺地区之普定卫。

俗尚鬼号，正祭者为鬼主。唐开成初（836年），鬼主阿凤内附。会昌中（841—846年），封罗甸王。后唐天成二年（927年），罗甸王普露请率九部入贡。宋开宝间（968—975年），有普贵者纳土归附，仍袭王爵，自济火至普贵，凡三十六世矣。时有宋景阳者，真定人，[①]奉诏平定诸蛮。因析置大万谷落总管府授之。元开置安抚、长官分授诸酋长。

明朝洪武四年（1372年），有霭翠、[②]宋钦及土人安沙溪等归附。诏以霭翠为贵州宣慰使，钦与沙溪等俱同知；皆设治于会城内，仍各统所部，居水西，而霭翠最强。霭翠死，弟安的[③]袭职，因为安氏。安氏领罗夷民四十八部，部长曰头目。宋氏世居卫城侧，领夷民十二部，部长曰马头。同知安氏领夷民一部，部长亦曰头目。

安氏世据水西之地，南逾陆广，[④]东接遵义，[⑤]西连赤水，[⑥]北抵永宁，[⑦]延袤数百里，山险箐深，有水西、大方、[⑧]织金、[⑨]火灼

---

① 真定，今之正定。

② 霭翠在元朝身兼四川行省左丞、顺元宣慰史之职。见《炎徼纪闻》卷三。

③ 田汝成《炎徼纪闻》谓，霭翠由其妻继承，后霭翠幼弟安匀继承之，并未提及安的。此处恐顾祖禹有误。

④ 陆广，陆广河岸一城镇，在贵州修文地区。陆广河为水西最大之河流。它起自普定东，流经修文，汇入乌江。

⑤ 遵义，清朝名。

⑥ 赤水，今毕节县，明时称为赤水卫。

⑦ 永宁，今四川叙永地区，元朝称永宁路，明朝称永宁卫。

⑧ 大方地，在今大定地区，时在水西之西部，靠近毕节卫。

⑨ 织金城，水西之西北地带。

诸城堡①，而大方尤为险固；役属部落日以富强。

万历中（1573—1619 年），安疆臣潜与播酋②相结，继而朝廷赫然，诛播，③惧祸及，遂悉力深入，播平；朝廷嘉其功，不问也。

天启初（1621 年），疆臣死，子安位幼弱，土目安邦彦挟之以叛。时永宁贼奢崇明④者亦倡乱，与邦彦相结。朝廷讨之，崇明败，归邦彦。又，乌撒土目安效良，⑤霑益⑥土目李贤等皆叛，应邦彦。邦彦纵横滇黔之交，南犯会城，东袭偏沅，⑦洪边⑧土司宋万化及东西诸苗悉叛，应之。官军四面攻讨未克。

天启四年（1624 年）督臣朱燮元议以滇兵出霑益，遏乌撒应援，而别布天生桥、⑨寻甸，⑩以绝其走。蜀军临毕节，⑪扼其交

---

① 火灼城，今黔西县之北，亦称火灼堡，或火著。

② 播酋，即杨应龙，公元 1595–1601 年率部反叛。唐时，杨的祖先始为播州首领，夺取南诏领土，杨应龙已是第二十九代首领。从其始祖至杨应龙，统治已近八百年。见《明史》卷三二一。

③ 明朝廷震怒，遣远征军征之，击败杨，并诛之。

④ 明朝时期，奢氏家庭为川黔边境一大彝族家族。永宁在今关岭县境。

⑤ 乌撒，靠近云南镇雄、贵州威宁。《元史·地理志》"乌撒者蛮名也。其部在中庆东北七百五十里，旧名巴凡兀始，今曰巴的甸，自昔乌杂蛮居之。今所辖部六，曰乌撒部、阿头部、易溪部、易娘部、乌蒙部、闷畔部。其东西又有芒布、阿晟二部。后乌蛮之裔折怒始强大，尽得其地。因取远祖乌撒为部名。宪宗征大理，累招不降，至元十年（1273 年）始附，十三年立乌撒路。"乌撒是彝族。随安疆臣反叛者安效良。

⑥ 霑益，云南东，唐时为播、剌部落占，此部可能操掸语。南诏治下，此地为摩弥部落所占，摩弥可能与彝族同源。与这次反叛有关的头目乃李贤。

⑦ 偏沅，沅州、偏桥关之合称。明朝，偏沅巡抚受命管理苗族事务，在沅州、偏桥关驻留各半年。清朝废之。明时它为中国西南最重要地区之一。

⑧ 洪边，元朝首次建立，贵阳以北约 4 公里处。反叛首领名宋万化。

⑨ 天生桥，贵州安顺县西北，乃战略要地。

⑩ 寻甸，在云南。明时，称为寻甸军民府，后称寻甸府。

⑪ 毕节，贵州西北、川滇黔间之重要商业中心。

通四出之路，而别出龙场、①岩头，以夺其险。黔兵由普定②渡思腊河经趋邦彦巢，而陆广、鸭池，③捣其虚。粤西出泗城，④分兵策应。然后率大军由遵义鼓行而进。燮元旋以忧去。

崇祯二年（1629年）燮元复督川湖云贵广五省之兵，再涖黔。乃檄滇兵下乌撒，蜀兵出永宁、毕节，扼其各要害，而自帅大军驻陆广，逼大方。会邦彦与奢崇明犯赤水，深入永宁。乃遣官军一从三岔⑤入，一从陆广入，一从遵义入，复以奇兵绕其后，贼不能支，遂大溃，斩邦彦等。围安位于大方，贼窘，请削水外六目地及开毕节等驿路以降，许之。燮元又遣兵诛摆金、两江、巴乡、狼狈、火烘五峃叛苗，⑥以孤其势。位寻死，其族党争纳土归附。燮元因请分水西之壤、投诸渠长及有功汉人，使势少力分，易以制驭。于是水西复定。（卷一二三，贵州，四）

在上述之部落诸头人中，安氏和奢氏家族确系彝族，而宋、李二氏，则难判定其是否彝族。可断定者，彝族头人辖下之诸多部落，并非彝族。通过这段记载我们可以看出明代为平定彝族付出了何等巨大的努力——以督臣率五省兵力，始获成功。此在多大程度导致其

① 龙场，今贵州之修文县。
② 普定，贵州安顺地区属地。
③ 鸭池河，为陆广河上游一支流。
④ 泗城，今广西凌云地区。民国废之。
⑤ 三岔，即三岔寨，普定北。
⑥ 此五部今不能判定，似为地名。

最后垮台，难以确评；然1644年明朝之覆灭，此乃为一大因素无疑。

清朝治下，水西安氏彝族仍然强大。康熙三年（1665年），吴三桂征服安坤，①将其领地划分五府。安坤之妻逃至乌蛮，生一子名安世宗。②后清廷决定不以朝官治理，安世宗于1683年被委任为宣慰使。1792年，总督王继文上奏，称安世宗理政不善，当应革除。故而安世宗之职被夺，其辖地复为朝廷官员控制。

《炎徼纪闻》对水西地区之彝族，描述极佳。此为田汝成于1560年所撰。田汝成乃中国西南一位高级官吏，有十余年处理土著部落事务之经验。该书为后代研究者广泛引用；然书中所述彝族史实，则常被人忽视。

> 罗罗本卢鹿而讹。为今称有二种。居水西、十二营、③宁谷、④马场、⑤漕溪者为黑罗罗，亦曰乌蛮。居慕役者为白罗罗⑥，亦曰白蛮。风俗略同，而黑者为大姓。罗俗尚鬼，故又曰罗鬼。
>
> 蜀汉时有火济者，从丞相亮破孟获有功，封罗甸国王，即今宣慰使安氏远祖也。自罗甸东西，若自祀、夜郎、牂牁，则以国名；若特磨、⑦白衣、九道，则以道名，皆罗罗之种也。罗

---

① 《清史稿·土司传》。

② 《清史稿·土司传》。

③ 十二营，贵州镇宁北15公里，清朝废之。

④ 宁谷，贵州安顺西南15公里，清朝废之。

⑤ 马场，贵州平越沿马场河之一地名。

⑥ 慕役，关岭南约30公里，元时为一寨子，明清时为长官司。

⑦ 特磨，云南之广南地区属，宋朝称特磨道。

罗之俗，愚而恋主，即虐之，赤族尤举其子姓，若妻妾戴之，不以为仇。故自火济至今，千有余年，世长其土，勒四十八部。部之长曰头目。其人深目长身，黑而白齿，椎结跣躈，荷毡戴笠①而行，腰束苇索，左肩拖羊皮一方，佩长刀箭箙。富者以金钏约臂。悍而喜斗，修习攻击，雄尚气力。宽则以渔猎、伐木为业；急则屠戮相寻，故其兵常为诸苗冠。谚云："水西罗鬼，断头掉尾。"言其相应若率然也。

亦有文字，类蒙古书者。坐无几席，与人食，饭一盘，水一盂，匕一枚，抄饭哺客，抟之若丸，以匕跃口，食已，必涤噱刷齿以为洁。作酒盎而不缩，以苇管啐饮之。男子则髡发而留髻。妇人束发，缠以青带，烝极旁通；觋不恶也。父死收其后母，兄弟死则妻其妻。新妇见舅姑不拜，裸而进盥，谓之奉堂。男女居室，不同帷第，潜合如奔狼，而多疑忌相贼也。白罗罗之俗略同。而饮食恶草，盛无盘杯，爨以三足釜，灼毛䐦血。无论鼠雀省蚔蝝蠕动之物，攫而燔之，攒食若凴。不通文字，结绳刻木为信。女子以善淫名者，则人争取之以为美也。人死以牛马革裹而焚之。居普定者为阿和，俗同白罗，以贩茶为业。(《炎徼纪闻》卷四)

有关唐以前之黔西、滇东北之记载，颇为不足。此乃多山、偏

---

① 竹丝编制之锥形帽。

僻之地，汉族之影响几未越出犍为、朱提①（今宜宾）之西南境外。从唐至今，川滇主要通道沿此地区以东，经叙永、毕节、霑益而昆明。②《蛮书》称之为北路。自晋代开始（265年），此地之居民被称之为爨。"当天宝中，东北自曲靖州，③西南至宣城，邑落相望，牛马被野，在石城、昆州、曲轭、晋宁、喻献、安宁至龙和城，谓之西爨。在曲靖州、弥鹿川、升麻川、南至步头，谓之东爨"。④

据《蛮书》所载，石城⑤为味县故地，距今曲靖15英里。龙和城位于大理以东。故而西爨所据之地，约从今之曲靖向西至大理。唐之曲州、靖州，与今四川之庆符、长宁南紧连。弥鹿大致相当于今之泸西县。升麻位近今之曲靖。步头无确考，似在今红河畔之建永县南。⑥故而东爨之域，为长江以南宜宾南至越南边境之广阔地区。

人们通常视爨为彝族。东爨乃彝族无疑。《蛮书》所述可证之。西爨则不然。他们属于白蛮，其语言、文化均不同于东爨。唐朝后期，东爨、西爨均为南诏国辖属。南诏王阁罗凤（748—749年）迫西爨两万家族迁居永昌地区。东爨则散逃山区，以免遭西爨之命运。

---

① 朱提，朱读如殊，提，上支反。

② 此为《蛮书》所定之地名，尚待考订。然该书卷一称，沿此路所居者，卢鹿，及与罗罗有关之部落。例如："过鲁望第七程至竹子岭，岭东有暴蛮部落，岭西有卢鹿蛮部落。第六程至生蛮磨弥殿部落。此等部落，皆东爨乌蛮也。男则发髻，女则散发。见人无礼节拜跪，三译四译乃与华通，大部落则有鬼主……"

③ 唐朝无曲靖之名。此处应读为曲州、靖州。曲州，靠近今庆符；靖州位于四川旧叙永。

④ 《蛮书》卷四。

⑤ 《蛮书》卷二："石城川，味县故地也。贞观中为郎州。开元初改为南宁州。州城即诸葛亮战处故地也。"

⑥ 建水县，即旧临安府。有关步头之考证，见 Pelliot, "Deux itinéraires de Chine en Inde", *BEFEO* 4, 138.

后东爨扩及西爨故地。①

爨之起源，尚待研究。西爨自称其祖先晋时居山西安邑地区。②此传说与事实不符，从公元三世纪起，爨为云贵统治家族之一。诸葛亮遣军征战云南，移黑羌万户入川，而将其赢弱者分配给大姓为部曲，爨即为此种大姓之一。③或许因此大姓日益强大，汉族乃以其名称呼其治下所有之部族。爨之统治家族是否为汉族之后裔，难以论定，因此传说包涵之内容极少。唐朝以后，不复使用爨之称呼。

论者常以云南之彝族为爨。中国古书称彝文为爨文，然视所有之爨均为彝族，则不甚确切。爨为公元四至十世纪常用之政治名称。在此期间，爨或许指许多极不相同之土著落族。东爨名为南诏所辖，实有颇大之独立性。

明朝期间，东爨在四川所占据之地，唐时分属四个军民府，即乌蒙、乌撒、东川、镇雄是也。据《明史》，④此地之居民乃唐时称为乌蛮之"罗罗"后裔。历史记载亦表明，宋时一彝族头人获乌蛮王头衔，元朝授与此地区头人为宣慰使衔。其中最重要者为乌撒，故有一专门官吏留驻其间。明初，此地区为汉族征占，然极不成功，叛乱时

---

① 《蛮书》卷四："阁罗凤遣昆川城者杨牟利以兵围胁西爨，徙二十余万户于永昌城。乌蛮以言语不通，多散林谷，故得不徙……乌蛮种类，稍稍复振，后徙西爨故地。"亦见《新唐书·南蛮》下："阁罗凤遣昆川城使杨爨牟利以兵围胁西，徙户二十余万于永昌城，东爨以语言不通，多散依林谷，得不徙……乌蛮种复振，徙居西故地。"

② 《新唐书·南蛮》下："西爨自云本安邑人，七世祖晋南宁太守，中国乱，遂王蛮中。"《云南厅志》卷一八九称：晋时南宁太守之职。南宁在齐、梁时方设，然长官为刺史，非太守也。

③ 《华阳国志》卷四："（诸葛亮）……移南中劲卒青羌万余家于蜀，为五部。所当无前，军号正……分其赢弱配大姓焦雍晏爨孟量毛李为部曲。"

④ 《明史》卷三一一："东川芒部诸夷，种类皆出于猡猡。厥后子孙蕃衍，各立疆场，乃异其名曰东川，乌撒，乌蒙，芒部，禄肇，水西。无事则互起争端，有事则相为救援。"

部民常助其水西之亲属。

　　吴三桂为满族人占据了此地。后吴又反叛，清廷不得不再度征服之。雍正年间（1723—1735年）总督鄂尔泰①奏请废土司之地方自治政权，尔后由流官取代之。故所有土司起而反叛。统治者以血腥屠杀镇压叛乱，大批彝族被杀。今此地几无彝族余存，盖因于此。

　　最后，大凉山西北之建昌河谷，乃仅存之独立之彝族聚居地。汉朝时期，此河谷之北部称邛都。元鼎六年（前111年），此地开为越巂郡。后汉、晋、刘宋和齐朝，沿袭称之。后周改其名为西宁州，继而名为严州。咸通三年（863年），此地为南诏所并，南诏始称其为建昌，引黑蛮、白蛮入。但黑蛮、白蛮是否为彝族，实不可知。在宋朝，承继南诏之大理国，对此地失去控制，故此地内乱频繁。蒙古族征服云南，土司均投降。明朝并此地，更名为建昌卫。②

　　沿建昌河谷为一通往中国西南及其以远区域之主要通道。此即诸葛亮远征之路。历朝均尽力使之畅通，然成功之时甚少，即使唐朝时也仅能在短期内维持此道。此地河谷、山麓之彝族，为汉族统治者所屈服，并在其地设治。

　　有关大凉山彝族之资料甚少。可能直至清末此地之彝族仍保持了独立。在雍正（1723—1735年）、嘉庆（1796—1820年）年间，数次力图降服此地彝族，但显然没有成功。彝族各部不断袭击汉族统治者，掳去不少汉族人丁充当奴隶。约在同治三年（1869），贵州提

---

① 《清史稿》卷五一四、卷五一五。
② 朝代更换，地名随之而变者，常也。新名为建昌卫。

督周达武率部入大凉山核心地区，释放成千之汉族俘虏。本世纪初，赵尔丰奏请清廷，欲彻底征服山区之彝族，旋因1908年光绪去世而搁置。此后不久，彝族杀死一英国传教士，赵尔丰乃从东北、西南两路，夹攻其地。两军汇聚山区，赵尔丰乃得以辟一通道，横贯此地，沿途要塞驻扎军队。赵尔丰禁止黑彝畜奴，废土司制，建立汉族统治。所以临近清朝覆亡之际，因巴贝尔（Baber）、多隆（Dollone）之介绍而闻名于世的"独立倮倮区"，最后屈服了。[1]

彝族所居三个重要地区之历史梗概，从汉文资料中所能窥其貌者，大致如是。关于彝族文化之特殊表规，下略述之。

除头人家族外，彝族与其邻居相比，物质文化较为落后。他们为半畜牧民族，然并不挤奶饮用。凡有奴隶之地农业即为奴隶所事，而奴隶者几不能以彝族称之。彝族之房屋，乃竹篱板舍。他们几无家具可言，仅有之器皿，惟几只略事加工之木碗、竹篓和铁锅。

彝族所知之调味品仅盐一种，此乃昂贵之奢侈品。其仅有之纺织品，乃粗制原始之麻织品，及用作大氅之粗毡。彝族既无货币，亦无度量衡。他们没有陶器，这一特点与古代当地之居民相似。《蛮书》称，南诏无陶器，所用则金银器皿及竹单。[2]

彝族之羊毛毡氅，为其独有。毡质粗糙而不均匀，其色有褐、蓝或羊毛本色。彝族男女，冬夏皆不离身。毡氅又是床垫、毯子，乃至充作屋顶。此物在《蛮书》中即有记载：

---

① 《清史稿》卷五一三。
② 《蛮书》卷八："南诏家食用金银，其余官将用竹单。贵者饭以筯，不匙。贱者，搏之而食。"

其蛮丈夫一切披毡，其余衣服略与汉同，唯头囊特异耳。南诏以红绫，其余向下皆以皂绫绢。其制度取一幅物，近边撮缝为角，刻木如樗蒲头，实角中，总发于脑后为一髻，即取头囊都包裹，头髻上结之。羽仪已下及诸动有一切房甄别者，然后得头囊。若子弟及四军罗苴已下，则当额络为一髻，不得戴囊角，当顶撮髽髻。并披毡皮，俗皆跣足。（武英殿聚珍版）

唐朝之南诏，口操掸语。今之掸族，一般不用毯子，尤不使用毡氅。

彝族著名之"天菩萨"，乃发式之一种。其法系将头发前梳，编织缠绕于前额，使其突出成角状。中国西南各族，均无以此方式梳发者。《蛮书》载，南诏之低级官员、武士乃着此饰。此可能因南诏大多数军士系由彝族组成。

在印度曼尼普尔（ManiPur）之那加诸部落中，有一部落之发式与彝族相同。[1] 由于亚洲其它民族无此发式，故两者之巧合，决非偶然。据说有一种彝族传说，其祖先来自该地区，但此说尚难肯定。

彝族文化之另外两个特征，即葬礼和祭祀，亦应作一简单介绍。

概而论之，所有的民族之宗教信仰都是守旧的，其中尤以丧礼为最。彝族周围均为信佛教的民族，然这些民族之信仰、行为对他们毫无影响。基督教传教士之努力，亦未能起作用。彝族因长期抵制外

---

[1] T.C.Hodson, *The Naga Tribes of Manipur*; 1911, pp.29–30.See also the plate facing p.21.然如缠绕之发乃辫之，则北方诸民皆尚此, Cf.Kurakichi Shiratori, The Queue among the Peoples of North Asia, *Mem. Toyo Bunko*, No.4.

来影响，其葬礼颇具古代遗风。彝族行火葬，此与中国之其它土著截然不同。早在唐朝，汉文史书即有此记载。《蛮书》谓：

> 蒙舍及诸乌蛮不墓葬。凡死后三日焚尸，其余灰烬掩以土壤，唯收两耳。南诏家则贮以金瓶，又重以银，为函盛之，深藏别室，四时将出祭之。其余家或铜瓶、铁瓶盛耳藏之也。[①]

乌蛮包括彝族之祖先东爨。彝族不保存双耳，惟行火葬，此为访问过这个地区的马哥·波罗所证实："人民焚其尸，取其骨置盒中，悬于崖穴内，避人畜及之也。"[②]

人们多认为南诏即"掸"，然"掸"为语言集团，非种族集团也。今之掸族不火葬死者，尽管在佛教及印度教影响之下，他们仍行土葬，此可能表明，在文化上南诏与彝族之关系，较今自称南诏是其祖先之掸族，更为密切。或则说明南诏之大部分臣民，均系彝族。《蛮书》又称：

> 白爨及白蛮，死后三日埋殡，依汉法为墓，稍富室，广栽杉松[③]。

[①] 《蛮书》卷八。

[②] E C.Baber, "China in some of Its Physical and Social Aspects", *Proeedings of the Royal Geographic society*, n.s, v, 1883, pp.445–48, identifies the Coloman of marco polo with the Lolo, in which he is probably correct. 巴贝尔视马哥·波罗所说之"科罗人"乃"罗罗"，此说可能正确。

[③] 《蛮书》卷八。

此亦黑、白蛮在文化上之差异。

《新唐书》称：

> 夷人尚鬼（祖先？——作者），谓主祭者为鬼主，每岁户出一牛或一羊，就其家祭之。送鬼迎鬼必有兵，因以复仇云。①

上述各种历史、传说上之史料，均与彝族起源之理论有关。拉古柏里（Lacouperie）立论最早，②谓，彝族乃古代西藏东北之民族向东南扩张而来。拉古柏里氏把中国古书上之氐羌与彝族相连，然其并未出据支持此论，故待讨论丁文江氏之理论时再述。

维尔（Vial）及其他学者，试图从语言学角度论证彝族与藏族有关。可惜此种立论的根据，全在于仰赖精选有限之词汇进行比较。根据我们对藏族的语言原则的了解，这两种不同的语言，是很难精确地概括在一起的。

丁文江氏乃第一个实地调查者。他将自己的理论奠基于体质及历史的事实之上。③他在云南旅行时曾测量了许多彝族居民，所获得的大部头部指数乃长头型。丁氏断定："在历史上，倮罗与羌族结合，在四川西北、青海、南疆，形成一重要之部族。在南疆，他们与

---

① 见《新唐书·南蛮》下。同样之习俗以前雅库特人亦有。见 W. Jochelson, Kumniss Festivals of the yakut, *Boas Aniversary Volume*, 1906, p.263.

② Op.cit., pp.480–81. Vial, *Les Lolos*, 1898. 亦见 J.Deniker, *Races of Man*, 1900, pp.381–382, and H.R.Davies, *Yunnan*, p.337.

③ 丁文江：《云南之土著部落》，《中国医学杂志》1921年3月号。

名为月支的伊朗族通婚。伊朗血统又通过羌族而影响了倮罗。"丁氏所用伊朗一词，似与里普利（Ripley）之观念相同。

丁氏在其后来著作中宣称，他测量之彝人，多系白彝。是以丁氏之发现，乃不足为奇。[1]长头型的因素与狄克森（Dixon）之里海型相一致，[2]此种因素在白彝中占第二位。由于白彝乃是臣服于黑彝之民族集团，故长头因素或许体现了古老的孟—高棉族之血缘。[3]狄克森以吕真达（Legendre）之测量为其分析之基础，然此测量表明占优势者乃短头型。丁氏、吕真达调查彝民之数目均有限，不足以证明其推论。

将假定的彝族的某些高加索特征，归之于通过月氏传入的伊朗血缘，实为牵强附会。实则，月氏之族属至今尚无定论，但大多数人均认为他们乃印度—斯基泰人。[4]《前汉书》中之片断材料记载，[5]月氏为敦煌、祁连间一游牧民族，约在公元前三世纪末被匈奴打败，其中之大部分向西迁徙，征服了曾经推翻希腊人巴克特利亚王国（大夏）之塞种人。在公元初，月氏人征服印度西北，后在此建贵霜帝国。少数未西迁之月支氏，则向西南移动，与羌族混居；汉族将匈奴逐出今新疆东部后，小月氏被劝重归故地。

---

[1]　见《漫游散记（云南之行）》，《独立评论》1933年，34—36号。

[2]　R. B. Dixon, *Racial History of Man*, p.281. L. Kilborn and R. Morse 两人最近测量了彝人，其结果尚未公诸于世。

[3]　Dixon, op.cit., p.276：普侬、摩伊、卡及其它孟–高棉语族人，有明显的长头特征。

[4]　此论近有探讨。见 Sten Konow, Kharoshthi Inscriptions, *Corpus Inscriptionum Indicarum 2*, Pt.I, 1929, pp.510–522.

[5]　《前汉书》卷九五。

　　人们常将此期间中亚之一切事情，皆与月氏联系。事实上，月氏是否曾到达四川，殊难肯定。历史上彝族有向北迁徙之举，假若夜郎为彝族之祖先，则月氏迁徙之时，他们早已定居于南方。

　　巴克斯顿（Buxtun）之理论，[①]基于丁文江氏的测量及詹弥森（Jamieson）提供的资料。詹弥森坚持彝族来自藏缅边界，因为他们是中国西南唯一畜马之人。[②]故而巴克斯顿把彝族与他的黑亚细亚族相联，此即埃利奥特·史密斯（Elliot smith）之褐色种族，他们曾横跨西亚到达地中海。此论与丁文江之理论不同，因巴克斯顿系将彝族与南方喜马拉亚山麓之民族相联系。尽管吕达真之测量较丁氏所测重要，然丁文江、巴克斯顿均未重视他的结果，而巴克斯顿则对所研究对象的历史事实不甚熟悉。

　　彝族传说，谓其起源于藏缅边境，其先民与汉族首次接触之地系在云南东北部。近有关于这一地区的有趣报道。昭通地区平原上有许多引人注意的土丘，"其中一些已被发掘，土丘之内，有粗糙而未经加工之石头，显然作门框之用。又有烧制之特大砖块，上有特殊之花纹"。[③]以此推论它与彝族之起源有何关系，为时尚早。但此地之彝族流传，土丘乃彝族到此之前濮人所筑，后濮人为彝族所并。

　　彝族传说，他们并非大凉山之土著。在汉族夺其富裕河谷之后，方陆续逃至山区，此过程持续到1727年。此传说虽不可全信，

---

①　Buxton, *The Peoples of Asia*, pp.156–157.

②　Jamieson, "The Aborigines of Western China", *China Journal of Art and Science 1*, p.381.

③　C.C.Hicks, "The Nou Su", *Chinese Recorder 41*, p.211.

然彝族非当前所居之地的土著，似无疑义。①

黑、白之分，也许与所论之问题有些关联。用黑色一词表示高贵血统，在东北亚各族中普遍存在。耶律大石所建西辽国，自称黑契丹。此暗示百姓臣民乃原始契丹人。蒙古人自始就分黑白。成吉斯汗及其文武大臣，均属黑蒙古人。这可能说明彝族与北方文化有联系。彝族使用毡子、古代爨人之鬼魂祭祀，均说明同一问题。至于彝族火葬之来源，尚难以推测。此不能归之于佛教或印度教之影响，而在驱邪典礼上用火，却是一广泛存在的习俗。

彝族缺陶器，亦表明与北方有关。因历史上只有少数几个民族不用陶器，其中就有蒙古人。意味深长的是，尽管彝族周围之民族均用陶器，而彝族独无。

然彝族又如汉族，非饮用奶品之民族。亚洲的民族可分成比邻而居的两大集团，即食奶者与不食奶者。东北亚之通古斯人，蒙古人，土耳其人，藏族，伊朗人，近东各族及部分原始亚洲人，属食奶民族。汉族，日本人，掸族，彝族以及大多数孟—高棉人，均不食奶。在此情况下，彝族之不食奶，决非偶然。他们拥有牧群，然并不挤奶，倘彝族为原始牧民，失此重要文化特征，极不可能。②此亦不能视为受汉族之影响，因彝族一贯反感外来影响。

彝族之另一些特征，又表明与南方有关，如赤足行走，使用毒

---

① E. C. Baber, "Travels and Researches in the Interior of China", *Royal Geographic Society, Supplementary Papers*, I. P. 121. D'0I–l one, op, cit., p.107.

② 雅库特人在最不利环境下仍保留牧群。见 Jochelson, op. cit., pp.257–271.

箭，头上之"天菩萨"。然东南亚之典型武器弩，彝族中却未发现。

以上之讨论，使我们难于下一肯定之结论。一些事实表明某一倾向，另一些事实则截然相悖。现今之一些理论，仅据其中某一事实而得出。如果考虑到东南亚少数民族之复杂性，以及缺乏由训练有素之调查者作出的报道，很显然，必须先作大量的工作，方能得出准确的分类。

（原载《冯汉骥考古学论文集》，
文物出版社，1985 年，第 178—190 页）

俫倈与东爨

俫倈文旧称爨文，故俫倈，亦有称之作爨人者，但俫倈是否爨人或与爨人之关系如何？兹为略论之。

"爨"一字之最早见者，则为《华阳国志》。其中之南中志言"诸葛亮平南中，移南中劲卒青羌万余家于蜀……分其赢弱配大姓焦、雍、娄、爨、孟、量、毛、李，为部曲"，又言亮受其俊杰建宁爨习朱提孟炎及获为官。南中志又言"建宁郡之同乐县，大姓爨氏"。是知爨乃当时之大姓，既非种名，亦非国号也。现在所保存之大小爨碑，爨龙颜碑在陆凉，爨宝子碑在曲靖，均在云南境。前者作于刘宋大明二年，后者作于晋安帝义熙元年。二碑均用汉文，而爨龙颜碑之书者为爨道庆。是知爨姓不一定为夷姓，亦可为汉姓，至少其汉化之程度实甚深也。

爨之成为一种民族称号，或国号，约在隋唐之际。隋唐时其中又分东西，故有东西两爨蛮之称。《新唐书》言"西爨自言本安邑人，七世祖晋南宁太守，中国乱，遂王蛮中"。故有人以为僰㑩原为来自西北，而西欧学者如 Terriende Dacoupepie 辈，更张大其词，以为中国境内民族向西南迁移之张本。《云南通志》则驳《新唐书》之在晋时无南宁之名，南宁于齐梁时始有之，而官阶又非太守而为刺史。

爨人所居之地，为现在之四川南部、贵州之西部以及云南。《蛮书》言："西爨，白蛮也。东爨，乌蛮也。当天宝中，东北自曲靖州，西南至宣城，邑落相望，牛马被野。在石城、昆川、曲轭、晋宁、喻献、安宁至龙和城，谓之西爨。在曲靖州、弥鹿川、升麻川南至步头，谓之东爨。"

据《蛮书》，"石城川，昧县故地也。贞观中有郎州，开元初改为南宁州，州城既诸葛亮战处故地也"。其地距今曲靖22.5公里，龙和城在今大理以东。故西爨所居之地，约在今曲靖以西至大理之间。曲靖州在唐时，当为曲州靖州，自四川之庆符长宁以南之地，皆为唐时之曲州靖州。弥鹿约当现在之庐西县，升麻亦在曲靖以东。步头在于何地？颇不易言。据《读史方舆纪要》及法人伯希和之考证，当为现今之建水县境（见冯承钧译伯希和著之《交广印度两道考》）。故东爨所居之地，约为自四川叙府以南至越南之边境。

现在均以爨人为僰㑩，但实有不尽然者，因东爨固属僰㑩，而西爨则非也。西爨在语言文化上均与东爨不同，而类分上亦异。东爨为乌蛮，西爨为白蛮，樊绰早已明言之矣。西爨为何种民族？据其自言，则为汉人，此言当不甚可靠。西欧学者则以西爨为现在居于缅甸之克伦（Karen）民族。如《蛮书》言"阁罗凤遣昆川城使杨牟利以兵围胁西爨，徙二十万户于永昌城。乌蛮以言语不通，多散林谷，故得不徙。……乌蛮种类，稍稍复振，后徙居西爨故地"。说者以为克伦族南移之先声，因克伦族亦自言系来自北方也。此虽可为一种解释，但无法证明。

东爨之为倮㑩，似可无疑义，蛮书所载，极为明显。"过鲁望七程至竹子岭，岭东有暴蛮部落。岭西有庐鹿蛮部落。第六程至生蛮磨弥殿部落。此等部落皆东爨乌蛮也。男则发髻，女则散发。见人无礼节拜跪，三译四译乃与华通，大部落则有大鬼主"。此为庐鹿之最早见，亦即"倮㑩"为其讹音。其所言鬼主之事，亦与后来言倮㑩者相因。庐鹿大概本为一强大部落之名，后乃用为倮㑩之总称。

此处所言之鲁望竹子岭等地名，均不可考。按自汉以来，由蜀通云南之道，大约有二。一为自雅安荥经越大相岭经西昌而入云南，此即所谓司马相如所开，武侯南征之路也。按诸葛亮南征之路线，说者颇多。《华阳国志》有言自安上县由水道入越巂之语。安上今不可考，又自蜀无水道可入越巂者，去夏在康定晤任晓庄先生谈及此事，任君言安上应为现在之沈村及冷碛，清时冷边及沈边土司驻牧地也，因自荥经以西皆系崇山峻岭，无处可设县，果如是，则武侯南征，并未经大相岭，乃系自荥经由小路出化林坪下之龙坝铺以达大渡河边之冷边及沈边。此路较之大相岭为平坦，且较捷（冷碛与沈村，在泸定下10余公里，虽沿大渡河可通汉源之富林，但不能行船，且全程不过50多公里），此为入南中之主要路线，亦即《蛮书》所称之南路也。再为由戎州（叙府）渡江南行经庆符、筠连、曲靖等处而至昆明，《蛮书》所谓之北路是也。大概樊绰所称之南路与北路，系从云南方面视之，不然一在西南，一在东南均南路也，何有南北之分。不过北路崎岖险阻，且生夷为患，梗阻之时多而通时少。所谓鲁望竹子岭等地，即在此道之中，自唐以来此道沿途，即为保倮活动之地。《明史·土司传》载明太祖遣傅友德、沐英等平云南而敕之曰："东川芒部诸夷种类，皆出于保倮，厥后子孙蕃衍各立疆场，乃易其名曰东川（云南会泽县境）、乌撒（云南镇雄、贵州威宁境）、乌蒙（云南昭通境）、芒部（云南镇雄县境乌蒙子芒部居此故号）、禄肇、水西（贵州境），无事则互起争端，有事则相救援。"关于乌撒等源流，《元史·地理志》言："乌撒乌蒙宣慰司，在本部巴的甸。乌撒者蛮名也，其部在中庆（今昆明治）东北七百五十里，旧名巴凡兀姑，今曰巴的甸。自昔乌蛮杂居之，今所辖部六，曰乌撒部、阿头部、易溪部、易娘部、乌蒙部、闷畔部。其东西有芒布阿晟二部，后乌蛮之裔折怒始强大，尽得其地。国取远祖乌撒为部名。宪宗征大理，屡招不降，至元十年始附，十三年立乌撒路，十五年为军民总管府。二十一年改军民宣抚司。二十四年升乌撒乌蛮宣慰司。"明平其地为乌蒙、乌撒、东川及雄镇四军民府。故以地望而言，隋唐时东爨所处之地，亦即后来保倮活动之中心区域也。

爨人在隋时为文帝所灭，唐时臣服于南诏。但西爨为白蛮，为南诏所贱视，东爨为保倮，与南诏为互为婚姻之族。大概保倮在西南民族中世为统治阶级，故虽臣于南诏，而尚能与之互为婚姻约（近凌纯声先生在《人类学集刊》上著有《唐代的乌蛮白蛮考》一文，言南诏属倮㑩族，其言甚辩，当另为文以论之）。倮㑩与南诏之关系，在当时颇为密切，南诏中之劲旅，亦多倮㑩为之。《蛮书》言"罗苴（音斜）子皆于乡兵中试入，故称四军苴子。戴光兜鍪，负犀皮铜鼓排，跣足，历险如飞，每百人罗苴佐一人管之。"又言"负排又从罗苴中拣入，无员数，南诏及诸镇下将军起坐不相离捍蔽者，皆负排也"。由此可见罗苴子在南诏军旅中之重要。罗苴与倮㑩自称之曰"罗苏"，极为相近。其所言之装束及跣足、历险如飞等语，又与现在之言倮㑩者，甚为相似也。

由此可见"爨"，在初并非一国号，亦非一种名，而为当时之一大姓，及至今日在宜宾一带尚有姓爨者。爨姓之为夷姓或为汉姓，今尚不甚了，不过在春秋时，土士亦有姓爨者。而在唐时西南民族中实少有用姓之习，如南诏命名，则为"父子以名相属"，即子名之首一字连父名之末一字，而不用姓，倮㑩至今尚有沿此习者。论者此为南诏属倮㑩族之证，然实不足为据。唐书所载"父子以名相属"为缅甸民族之特征，南诏倮㑩，或得之于彼等。又倮㑩受南诏之统治，倮㑩中此种命名之俗，或为转得之于南诏，亦未可知。如元人统治西南未久，而倮㑩酋豪中，即有"蒙古语式"之命名者，月鲁帖木耳是也。又倮㑩酋豪中之有姓氏，始于明初，水西安氏是也。故从唐宋以前，西南民族中无姓氏之习推之，爨亦可为汉姓，或汉化之夷姓，不过彼自言为安邑人，则未可为典据也。但无论如何，自魏晋而后，中原扰攘，爨氏以西南豪族而征服其他各民族，遂据有云贵，中土之人遂以爨人呼之，而爨则由族姓而变为国号而兼种号，此等现象，在西南民族中，实不乏实例。故爨人中所包括之民族，想至为复杂，倮㑩不过为其中之一种，东爨是也。

（原载《杂说月刊》1942 年 1 期）

冉駹与羌

　　"小麦青青大麦枯，①谁当获者？妇与姑。丈人②何在西击胡，吏买马，君具车。请为诸君鼓咙胡。'（桓帝初天下童谣）《后汉书·五行志》言："案元嘉中，凉州诸羌，一时俱反，南入蜀、汉，东抄三辅，延及并、冀，大为民害。命将出师，每战常负。中国益发甲卒，麦多委弃，但有妇女获刈③之也。'吏买马，君具车'者，言调发重及有秩者也。'请为诸君鼓咙胡'者不敢公言，私咽语。"

　　当两汉之时，现在川西北汶、茂之间，有一民族，史称之曰冉駹④，但冉駹系属于何种民族？因汉以后，即寂焉无闻，记载中未曾明言，故今人有以为系属嘉戎族者，但非确论也。今将个人考察所

---

① 原误作"大麦青青小麦枯"。
② 原误作"大人"。
③ 原误作"利"。
④ 原文"駹"字多阙，下文径补，不另注。

及，略为书而出之，作为研究民族史者之一种参考。

记载中最早之言冉駹者，当为《史记》卷一一六《西南夷列传》："自莋以东北，君长以十数，冉駹最大，其俗或土著、或移徒，在蜀之西。自冉駹以东北，君长以十数，白马最大，皆氐类也。"由此可知冉駹在秦汉时为川西北之大部落。所谓莋者，为现代汉源、天全一带之羌属部落，其称曰莋，大概因其作竹索桥而言也。白马约当今之甘肃之武都一带，其为氐，亦羌属也。但冉駹一名亦有分称者，如《史记·大宛列传》："乃令骞因蜀犍为发间使，四道并出：出冉出駹、出徙出邛僰，各行一二千里。"又《司马相如传》传喻蜀檄言："因朝冉从駹，定莋存邛。"□① 将冉与駹分举，或疑为二族者。但亦未必然。因往籍中往往因行文之便，割裂名词，以求工整，倘想（概？）② 其证据，吾人固不得谓其为两族也。

言冉駹者当以《后汉书》《华阳国志》为最详，《后汉书》卷八六《南蛮西南夷传》："冉駹夷者，武帝所开，元鼎六年以为汶山郡。至地节三年契人以立郡赋重，宣帝乃省并蜀郡，为北部都尉。其山有六夷、七羌、九氐，各有部落。其王侯颇知文书，而法严重。贵妇人，党母族。死则烧其尸。土气多寒，在盛夏冰犹不释。故夷人冬则避寒入蜀为佣，夏则违暑反其众邑。皆依山居止，累石为室，高者至十余丈，为邛笼。又土地刚卤，不生谷粟麻菽，唯以麦为资，而宜畜牧。有旄牛无角，一名童牛，肉重千斤，毛可为毦。出名马。有灵

---

① 原文模糊不清。

② 原文模糊不清。

羊可疗毒。又有食药鹿，鹿麚有^①胎者，其肠中粪亦疗毒疾。又有五角羊、麝香、轻毛、毨^②鸡、牲牲。其人能作旄毡、斑罽、青顿、毞毲、羊羧之属。特多杂药。地上咸土，煮以成盐，麐^③羊牛马食之皆肥，其西又有三河、槃于虏，北有黄石、北地、卢水胡，其表乃为徼外。"

《华阳国志》所载与此略同："汶山郡本属郡北部冉駹都尉，孝武元封四年（按当作元鼎六年）置，旧属县八，户二十五万……有六夷、羌胡、羌虏^④、白兰、峒^⑤、九种之戎。牛、马、旄毡、斑罽、青顿、毞毲、羊羧^⑥之属。特多杂药^⑦、名香。土地刚卤，不宜五谷，惟种麦。而冰多寒盛，夏凝冰不释。故夷人冬则避寒入蜀，庸赁自食，夏则避暑反落，岁以以常，故蜀人谓之作五百石子也。"

《后汉书》及《华阳国志》所言，其中有数种文化特征，可与现在居其地之羌人相比较，此虽不能定其种落所属，然其间必有密切之关系也。例如"死则烧其尸"，故可知冉駹有火葬之俗，而羌人之火葬，则行之甚早。如《吕氏春秋·义赏》篇言："氐羌之民，其虏也，不忧其系累而忧其死不焚也。"又《御览》卷七九四引《庄子》佚文云："羌人之死，燔而扬其灰。"《吕氏春秋》之作者固为与羌人

---

① "麚有"二字原阙。
② "毨"字原阙。
③ "麐"字原阙。
④ "羌"字原阙，据题襟馆本补。
⑤ "峒"字原阙。
⑥ "羧"字原阙。
⑦ "药"字原脱，据题襟馆本补。

开玩笑。但吾人由此可知火葬对于羌人信仰上之重要，死而不焚，其悲戚有甚于被虏而系累者。在民族学上所知，宗教信仰之传播与改变，极为不易，今羌与冉駹同此俗，其间必有相关者。又现代居其地之羌，约三十年，均举行火葬，今虽惑于汉人风水之说，少有举行。但每砦中之火坟（即一族共同焚尸之所）均宛然存在，火葬之仪式，其中之耆老均能道之。《后汉书》言"众皆依山居止，累石为室，高十余丈为邛笼"一层，凡曾至汶、茂者，类能道之。例如至汶川境，一过飞沙关，两岸半山羌村石室如砦，故汉人称之曰砦子，每砦累石为碉楼二三，高百余尺，远望之，有如工厂之烟囱，但无烟耳。此想，即所言之邛笼也。羌佣一事，蜀人知之最悉，即如现在，每届冬令，成都市上出现身着粗麻布衫，蓬头垢面，行中蹒跚，胸挂"包打水井"者，皆羌民也。此类羌人，多来自理县之九枯后笮□①及茂县之黑水等地，其打淘水井，乃近代之适应，以往并不如此，但为佣则一也。《华阳国志》谓"蜀人谓之作五百石子"一语，遍询之川人，无有能知者。又如"贵妇人，党母族"，有人释之谓系母系，但虽不□②可必，而现代羌人之尊重女子与母族，则相同也。即以上所举之数而言，羌人与冉駹之关系，即可了□③矣。

虽《后汉书》所言之"六夷、七羌、九氐"，《华阳国志》所言之"六夷、羌胡、羌虏、白兰峒④、九种之戎"，其名不可甚解（白兰

---

① 原文模糊不清。
② 原文模糊不清。
③ 原文模糊不清。
④ "峒"字原阙。

或系后来之白兰羌）。大概其所言之夷与戎，均系指羌而言，而汉代以前，羌则统名之曰"戎"也。《华阳国志》言："汶山曰夷，南中曰昆明，汉嘉、越巂曰笮，蜀曰邛，皆夷种也。"其曰夷、昆明、笮、邛者，实则皆羌也。

　　然则汶山郡之羌人，在秦汉时何以称之曰冉駹？是亦不难索解，冉駹之号，或为其酋豪之姓或名，当时不察，即以其为部落之号或种号。以酋豪之名或姓为种名之事，在羌族中颇为常见，如范史《西羌传》言："其俗氏姓无定，或以父名母姓为种号。"又如"研（无弋爱剑之玄孙忍之子）至豪健，故羌人中号其后为研种"，再如爱剑十三世孙名烧当"复豪健，其子族更以烧当为种号"，此即是东汉最慓悍之烧当羌也。冉駹之名，当亦不外此例也。

（原载《西方日报》1949 年 2 月 13 日第六版

《中国边疆》副刊第廿八期）

松理茂汶羌族考察杂记

1938年暑假，余得四川大学西南社会科学研究所的支助，只身前往松潘、理县、茂汶作羌民族考察，历时三月。次年夏，又担任教育部组织的川康科学考察团社会组组长，再次前往调查。现将两次搜集所得羌人材料若干，结合古代文献记载的有关历史情况，整理成文，以供研究羌民族问题之参考。

一、羌民族的历史

中国历史上所见之羌，其所占之地域颇广，北自陕西之南部，甘肃青海之东南，沿川藏边境，南至雅属及嘉定，此半月形之山地，均曾为羌民族居留之所。但二千余年以来，羌人北受匈奴等民族之侵袭，东南受汉民族之压迫，西受西藏民族之蹂躏，其未绝灭者，非向化于汉人，即变而为藏人，其所剩余者只四川西北之松、理、茂、汶数县之地而已。即此数县之中，亦非全为羌人，其沿河及交通便利之处，多为汉人，其西北，则又多为西番与嘉戎也（西番、嘉戎均属藏族）。

"羌"一名词之最早见者，莫若《竹书》《诗经》及《尚书》。《竹书纪年》：殷商成汤"十九年大旱，氐羌来宾"。又《诗·商颂·殷武》："自彼氐羌，莫敢不来享，莫敢不来王。"及《周书·牧誓》："……庸、蜀、羌、髳、微、卢、彭濮人；称尔戈，比尔干，立尔矛，予其誓。"此数处所记载，可相信之程度，自属可以商榷。其所言氐羌究为何民族，亦无从考见。不过终宗周之世，氐羌之名，不见于载籍。说者谓周戎，即后来之西羌。此说既难证明，然亦不能否认也。

西汉之世，羌族渐盛，北与匈奴相结，时为西南之边患，后经赵充国、冯奉世之讨伐，始稍平服，但未能绝也。王莽篡汉，收西羌地，置海西郡（今青海）徙罪人以实之。及莽败，羌族复据西海，时为边乱。

羌与戎，大概有相当之关系。《后汉书·西羌传》直以戎为羌，在周时则皆称之曰戎，或曰西戎。其他种之戎，亦不下十余种。说者谓周之世不言羌，或其讳言羌，因羌之字为"羊"与"人"，含有轻视之意。而周人讳之之原因，因周民族之一部分为羌，又与羌互通婚姻，因周之母族为姜，姜，即羌也。《后汉书·西羌传》："西羌之本，出自三苗，姜姓之别也。"此但可以聊备一解，不足以为典据也。

《西羌传》又言，羌之始祖，原出于戎，如"不知爰剑何戎之别也"。又《华阳国志》"有六夷，羌胡，羌虏，白兰峒，九种之戎"。是皆以羌为戎者。

按西汉之旧制，益州部置蛮夷骑都尉，梁州部置护羌校尉，幽州部置领乌桓校尉。皆持节领护，理其怨结，岁时循行，问所疾苦，又数遣使驿通动静，使塞外羌为吏耳目，州郡因此可得警备。东汉初，隗嚣利用羌兵，与汉相距。光武平嚣，置护羌校尉，以牛邯领之，西方之局稍定。其后马武平羌，因校尉不职，遂去其官，已而又以羌祸未靖，复立校尉。

东汉为历史上羌民族之全盛时期，亦为当时汉王朝统治最大之患。仅以光武之世而言，据《后汉书·光武纪》记载：建武十年（34年）十一月，"先零羌寇金城（金城郡故城在今兰州广武县之西南）、陇西，来歙率诸将击羌于五溪（《续汉书·郡国志》云陇西襄武县有五溪聚），大破之"。十一年（35年）四月，"先零羌寇临洮"。十月，"因陇西太守马援击破先零羌，徙至天水陇西扶风"。十二年（36年）十二月，"金城郡属陇西郡属参狼羌寇武都，陇西太守马援讨降之"。十三年（37年）七月，"广汉徼外白马羌豪率种人内属"。中元元年（56年）十一月，"参狼羌寇武都，败郡兵。陇西太守刘盱遣军救之，及武都郡兵讨叛羌，皆破之"。终东汉之世，其祸未尝稍戢。倾全国之兵，竭府库之财，经百战之苦，乃仅能克之，然不能终绝也（其事详载《后汉书·西羌列传》，可以详看）。故范晔尝叹"自西戎作逆，未有陵斥上国，若斯其炽也"。

魏晋南北之世，羌族仍盛，且有时为患更烈。因汉人每对于异族归降之后，每每迁之内地，以为可以同化于汉族，讵知其患，反及于中国腹地，转甚于未迁之时也。三国之时，羌人所居之地，接近蜀魏，二国争欲引为己援，羌人则坐收其利。司马氏灭蜀代魏，羌患稍舒，元康以后，贾后与八王之乱，接踵而起，中原板荡，西北异族，亦乘机而起，变成南北朝一百三十余年之扰攘局面。即外人所称为中国历史上之黑暗时代，亦即俗所谓五胡乱华者（五胡，匈奴、鲜卑、羯、氐、羌），氐羌亦各为其中之一也。

五胡十六国之中，所谓羌氐之族者，一为仇池之祖之略阳杨氏，一为前秦之祖之略阳苻氏，一为后凉之祖之略阳吕氏。以上三者，即历史上所称之氐族。氐与羌在史籍中虽属并称，而氐与羌之关系，实无从考见。羌之大部，则为南安姚氏，即后秦之祖也。其事迹均载在史传，兹不赘（仇池见《魏书·氐传》《北史·氐传》，前秦见《晋书·载记》，后凉见《晋书·载记》，后秦见《晋书·姚弋仲载记》）。又《北史》卷九六，列传八四，宕昌、邓至、白羌、党项等传，附国传，亦为有关氐羌之记载。

氐羌之族，自隋唐而后，则寂焉无闻，大抵其近中原者，多同化于汉族。西方之羌，因吐蕃之兴起，亦为其掩盖。因吐蕃强盛，征服其周围民族，中国史籍，乃尽以吐蕃名之，而不复分别之也。

现在之羌人，与历史上所见之羌人，其关系若何，自为待考见之问题。不过松理汶茂之羌民，决非完全由他处之羌人，因受汉人之压迫，而后徙居其地者，自可断言。现在松理汶茂之羌人，均有同样之悠久历史，不过其山岭阻绝，与汉人之交通较少，故吾人知之较迟耳。但现在之羌人，与历史上之羌人，自有其相当之关系，此与各地记载中可见之。

《后汉书》以为秦以后之羌，皆出自无弋爱剑："无弋爱剑者，秦厉公时为秦所拘执，以为奴隶，不知爱剑何戎之别也。后得亡归，而秦追之急，藏于岩穴中，得免。羌人爱剑，初藏穴中，秦人焚之，有景象如虎，为其蔽火，得以不死。既出，又与劓女遇于野，遂成夫妇。女耻其状，被发覆面，羌人因以为俗。遂俱亡入三河间。诸羌见爱剑不死，怪其神，其畏事之，推以为豪。河湟间少五谷，多禽兽，以射猎为事，爱剑教之田畜，遂见敬信，庐落种人，依之者日益众。羌人谓奴为无弋，以爱剑尝为奴隶，故因名之。其后世世为豪。至爱剑曾孙忍时，秦献公初立，欲复穆公之迹，兵临渭首，灭狄獠戎，忍季父卬畏秦之威，将其种人附落而南，出赐支河曲西数千里，与众羌绝远，不复交通，其后子孙分别，各自为种，任随所之，或为牦牛种，越巂羌是也。或为白马种，广汉羌是也。或为参狼种，武都羌是也。忍及弟舞，独留湟中，并多娶妻妇，忍生九子，为九种。舞生十七子，为十七种。羌之兴盛，从此起矣。"又言："自爱剑后，子孙支分，凡百五十种，其九种在赐支河首以西，及在蜀、汉徼北。"关于蜀郡徼外之羌，后汉亦列有数种："牦牛、白马羌在蜀、汉，其种别名号，皆不可纪知之也。建武十三年（36 年）广汉塞外白马羌豪楼登等，率种人五千余户内属，光武封楼登为归义君长。至和帝永元六年（94年）蜀郡徼外大牂夷种羌豪造头等率种人五十余万口内属，拜造头为邑君长，赐印绶。至安帝永初元年（107年）蜀郡徼外羌龙桥等六种万七千二百八十口内属。明年蜀郡徼外羌薄申等八种三万六千九百口，复举土内属。冬，广汉塞外参狼种羌二千四百口复来内属。"

以上所言蜀郡徼外之羌，其与汶山之羌有别。其所在之地大都在汶山郡之南，或其东北。汶山郡之羌，武帝时，其国名或种名，称曰冉駹。按《史记》（卷一一六）西南夷传言："自嶲以东北，君长以十数，徙（音斯，即后来之徙县）筰都（筰音才各反即后之沈黎郡）最大。自筰以东北，君长以十数，冉駹（师古曰今夔州开州首领多姓冉者，本皆冉种也，駹音龙）最大。其俗或土著或移徙。在蜀之西，自冉駹以东北，君长以十数，白马最大（阶州茂县汉白马氐地）。皆氐类也。此皆巴蜀西南外蛮夷也。"（《汉书》同）

《后汉书》（卷八六）《南蛮西南夷列传》所言较详："冉駹夷者，武帝所开，元鼎六年（前111年）以为汶山郡。至地节三年（前67年），夷人以立郡赋重，宣帝乃省并蜀郡，为北部都尉。其山有六夷七羌九氐，各有部落，其王侯颇知文书，而法严重。贵妇人，党母族，死者烧其尸。土气多寒，在盛夏冰犹不释。故夷人冬则避寒入蜀为佣，夏则违暑反其邑。众皆依山居止，累石为室，高十余丈为邛笼。又土地刚卤，不生谷粟麻菽，惟以麦为资，而宜畜牧。有牦牛无角，一名童牛，肉重千斤，毛可为毦（音冒）。出名马。有灵羊可疗毒。又有食药鹿，鹿麚有胎者，其肠中粪，亦可疗毒疾。又有五角羊、麝香、轻毛毷鸡、牲牲。其人能作旄毡、班罽、青顿、毞毲、羊羖之属，特多杂药。地有咸土，煮以成盐。麝羊牛马食之皆肥。其西又有三河槃于虏，北有黄石，北地卢水胡，其表乃为徼外。灵帝时复分蜀郡北部，为汶山郡云。"

此处所言之六夷、七羌、九氐，自然无从考见，而夷又为普通之名词，非民族之名词也。其言"贵妇人，党母族"，在现在之羌民中，犹有相当痕迹可寻。"死则烧其尸"一层，与过去三十年前，羌民中之埋葬风俗，完全相同，近则多学汉人之穴葬矣。"冬则避寒入蜀为佣"，羌人至今尚如此。成都市上之羌人，挂牌打井者，到处可见也。至于"累石为室，高者至十余丈为邛笼"语，则为羌民族居室之特征，非他民族所有者。故《后汉书》所记，虽已二千余年，尚可为现在汶理茂羌人之写照也。

《华阳国志》所言略同："汶山郡，本蜀郡北部冉駹都尉，孝武元封四年置，旧属县八，户二十五万……有六夷、羌胡、羌虏、白兰峒九种之戎。牛马、旄毡、班罽、青顿、毞毲、羊羖之属，特多杂药名香，土地刚卤，不宜五谷，惟种麦。而冰多寒，盛夏凝冻不释。故夷人冬则避寒入蜀佣赁自食，夏则避暑反落，岁以为常。故蜀人谓之作五百石子也。"

然汶山郡之羌人，在西汉时，何以称之曰冉駹？此亦不难索解。冉駹之号，或为其酋豪之姓或名，当时不察，即以之为其国号或种号。以酋豪之名或姓，为种名之事，在羌族中，亦颇常见。如范史言："其（指羌而言）俗世族无定，或以父名母姓为种号。"又如

"研（无弋爱剑之玄孙，忍之子）至豪健，故羌中号其后为研种"。又如爱剑十三世孙名烧当，"复豪健，其子孙更以烧当为种号"。冉駹之名，亦不外此例。《后汉书》言："其山（汶山郡）有六夷七羌九氐。"《华阳国志》亦言："有六夷羌胡羌虏白兰峒九种之戎。"其文虽不甚可解，大概此处之"夷"亦系指羌而言。如《华阳国志》言："汶山曰夷，南中曰昆明，汉嘉越巂曰筰，蜀中曰邛，皆夷种也。"其曰夷、昆明、筰、邛者，其实皆羌类也。

　　唐以前之各聚落之名，今多不可考。唐以后之名称，尚有流传至今者。如理番河（即沱江，又称杂谷脑河）两岸之羌人，唐时称白狗羌，如唐书："武德六年，白兰白狗羌遣使入贡，七年，以白狗等羌地，置维、恭二州。"维州即现在之威州也。恭州则不甚可考。又如当狗城，以其当白狗羌之路，故名。即广德二年（764年）剑南节度严武破吐蕃拔当狗城者是也。当狗城之遗址，在于某一地点，今已不可考。大抵总不出维州以西，沱江之下游也。又如笼山城，在唐时为羌中最强者之一，广德七年（769年），吐蕃陷维州笼山城即此也。今为笼山寨颇险要。又茂县城外之静州土司，家藏有唐代敕文，前不久方在1935年战乱中损毁，不胜惋惜。自宋元而后，各羌寨之名，均斑斑可考。因其过详，不能在此处讲述。

二、羌区之地理

羌地之山曰岷山，江曰岷江。岷山即汶山，《史记·封禅书》："自华以西，名山曰渎山。渎山者，汶山也。"《汉书》作嶓山，岷汶嶓，均可通。岷山亦即所谓西山之一部分。"蜀之险在西山，西山之险，州其要领也。"岷江者，即古代地理书中之所谓江源。《禹贡》"岷山导江"，《荀子》"江出于岷山，其源可以滥觞"者，古人不知金沙江，故以岷江为江源。岷江亦名汶江，亦曰都江，亦曰外水，岷江则通称也，

羌地之山穷水恶，则罕有其匹。自灌县而上，即无平地。清末时，有灌县人董玉书（湘琴）者，以戎马书生自负，后入松潘总兵夏毓琇幕，作《松游小唱》一词，词虽不甚工，而颇能描写，淋漓尽致。如其中写岷江沿河风景一段，云"松潘西望路漫漫，风景渐难看，河在中间，山在两边，九曲羊肠偏生跨在山腰半。抬头一线天，低头一束练，滩风响似百万鸣蝉，缠绵不断。最可厌，一山才断一山连，面目无更换，总是司空见惯。问蚕丛开国几经年，这沧桑如何不变"？

岷江水流之急，几沿河皆滩。其最浅之处，虽仅没胫，然亦不能涉而过也。其惟一交通，则惟缅索与索桥。如隔河仅数十步，有时如欲达彼岸，需绕行一日程或二日程方能达到也。岷江因其水流之急，故为一种极大之冲刷媒介，河床深至数千尺以上，两岸多系悬崖，甚少可种植之冲积河阶。

自映秀湾而上，石多土少。其岩石多片麻岩（gneiee）、片岩（shist），其他如花岗岩、石灰岩，亦甚普遍。不过因山势过陡，土壤均不能沾着，多随雨水冲刷以去，致成俗所谓"九石一土"之现象，气候南苦雨，而北苦旱。自娘子岭以至汶川县，雨降甚丰，故草木畅茂，山色秀丽。自汶川县城以上，则童山濯濯，岩石外露，不复见草木青葱之色矣。全年中最高温度为8月（30.52℃），最低温度为1月（0.3℃），最多雨者，为五六两月。每年落雨平均只38天。故气候甚佳，不若成都之平原之潮湿，及青甘之干燥也。其最高之山峰，终年积雪，四时不解，自10月初雪线开始下降，至1月则降至河谷。至次年三四月时低处之雪，方开始融解。故其农作之时间，由4月起至10月止。其地每日午时后必风，其原因乃由于河谷过深，上下气压不同之所致。

羌民族所居留之地，全为沿岷江河谷，及其支流之河谷。因河谷之地，海拔较低，故可耕种，再高则庄稼不能生长矣。沿岷江正流，近河床水边便为大路之地，多为汉人，或汉化之羌人。羌民所居之地，则为半山斜坡之上，再上则森林及草原带，人迹罕到。彼此间之交通极为不便，故称沟。

羌民对其环境之应适，可谓十分周到，虽汉民至其地者，亦不能不学羌民之办法。房屋即其一例也。

三、羌民之体质

羌人之体质，现在几无所知，华西大学之Morse医生，曾作不少之测量，但彼则将所测量之绝对数发表，未曾用统计方法，计算其恒数，故不能利用作比较。去年中央研究院曾派人在羌中测量近千人，但尚未能计算其结果。

以余个人之观测，羌人之体质，大体与汉人相同，而与西番及嘉戎稍异。但其中全无蒙古人式之眼折，亦一异事。羌人之体质，细察之可分为两部。即汶川理番为一部，茂县至松潘者为一部。汶川理番之羌人，体较高，但其特别惹人注意者，即为其勾形之鼻。此陶兰士所以谓羌人为东方之犹太人者。此种勾形之鼻，余初见之，颇不得其解。后至嘉戎地界，乃知其鼻形之由来，或者为如此。嘉戎之鼻高狭而长。羌人原有之鼻（于茂县松潘羌人中可以见之）低阔而短。若将高长之鼻，加之于低阔之鼻之上，即成勾形之状。故此种鼻形，并不需假设羌人为西方民族之迁于此者，而实为一种混合之鼻形也。

四、羌民族现在之人口

羌民族人口之确数，则毫无统计，茂县理番编制保甲村时均羌汉不分，混合计之，实不知其中羌人有若干，汉人有若干也。至土司所辖之地带，估计之数，亦不可得而知。据汶川县之保甲系统，羌人男1781人，女1721人，共3502人。此数目当然不能视为可靠。因保甲编制丁口时，多有隐匿之事，藉以避免差役，但无论如何，汶川县之羌人，至多不能超过5000以上也。余个人之印象及估计，现在所有之羌人，至多不过60000人，即茂县35000人，理番县20000人，汶川县5000人。此数目当然极不可靠，不过为一种猜测而已。

羌人人口，在近百年以来，减少之数，实为可惊。自经1935年战乱之后，若干羌寨，全被焚毁，其死于兵及瘟病者，又至少在1/10以上也。如汶川之萝葡寨，为羌人中最富庶之区，据言约百年前，其地有人口600余人，1935年前约400，以后只350余人而已。又黑虎七族，在明代及清初之时最为恶蠢，其变叛掠劫，几无岁无之。历官其土者，均不能制，其惟一绥靖方法，即为招抚。《四川通志》所载清康熙中茂县举人蒋复襄所作《招抚黑虎七族记》，可以概见。其中有言："历代以来，恃其山菁险阻，屡肆猖獗，而茂之黑虎生番尤甚。出没官道，掠掳我人民，□□我牲畜，岁无虚日。守土者议剿议抚，迄无成功，终明之世，未有能摄服者。"又《嘉庆四川通志》卷九十，武备志之边防志引《明史》云，宪宗成化九年，"松潘指挥金事尧彧志奏：……初黑虎寨最强，相传有神术，先知官兵，未至即遁去，或潜伏要害窃发，屡败我众，按察使龚独曰：我自不密耳，彼何能知。夜半密勒诸将绕兵进凡三十里，平明抵其寨，蛮大惊溃，斩缚各千人，得其首恶，余溃死无算，既而大征，破寨二十余，斩五百级，降者数千，皆编籍输粮"。（整理者按：此处所引之《明史》，非清代官修之正史，当别是一私家所著书）其丁口之多，可以想见。现在之黑虎寨则如何？一进黑虎沟，则满目荒凉，断井颓垣，触目皆是。即以黑虎之内五寨而言，原有居民600余户，至1935年之前，尚余200余户，以后则只余160余户，600余人而已。此不独黑虎羌人为然，七族亦如此。七族最盛时，有200余户。今则只余15户而已。羌人衰落之象可以想见。

羌民族中人口之减少，为一普遍现象，但此不独以羌民族为然。其他之原始民族，与其他高等文化民族接触时，亦莫不如此。

五、羌人之物质文化

羌人之物质文化，可分下列之数类说明之。

（一）屋宇及室内之用具

羌人之屋宇，其建筑之方法及样式，与汉人者大异。在中国境内之屋宇形式，甚至东亚之屋宇（蒙古人游牧之帐篷，另为一种，自当除外）可分为两大系：一为汉式之屋宇，二为羌藏式之屋宇。汉式之屋宇，大都类能知之，故不赘。羌式之屋宇，除羌人外，藏人西番及嘉戎中均用之。藏番及嘉戎之屋宇，与羌人者，虽不无小异，但皆属于一类。研究各种建筑物，其重要之点，在其样式，而不在建筑之原料。因原料系受自然环境之支配，而建筑样式，则多少受文化及历史背景之支配也。如羌人之建筑，均系石制，因其地片石甚多，俯拾即是，若烧砖为之，则反事倍而功半矣。他如萝葡岩片石甚少，其建筑之墙垣，则筑土为之，不过其版筑之方法，则与汉人稍异。

羌人之屋宇，几全为方形或长方形，通为二层，下层为牛羊豕圈上层住人，再上为平屋顶，大门开于正中之第一层，而楼梯则置于最后面，故登楼之时，必需经过牛羊圈之全部，其中黑暗秽臭，亟为可怖。全屋无第二门，所有人畜均由此门出入。问其何以如此，则曰"不紧慎"。第二层前面开小窗二，左右各一。故室中亟昏暗。室内生火时，此二小窗，亦为烟囱也。其接近汉人之地，大门则稍为改良。大门安置于第二层，门左有小平台一。先由独木梯上小平台，再右向而进大门。羌屋前面均有一小院，院与畜圈相通，人畜均由院门出入。院内及畜圈内，入秋时多置青草及小树枝之类，称曰"耗子"。厚约二三尺，牛羊豕践踏之，排泄亦于其中，经冬乃腐，第二年四月中乃出之以为肥料。对于羌人，此固一举而两得，但其秽臭，则实不堪言状。天晴则秽气熏人欲呕，遇雨则粪秽没胫。彼等处之，反泰然若无其事也。

关于大门开于第一层之屋宇，第二层前面为住宿之所，后面近楼梯处，为游息炊爨之处，中有一照壁隔开。大门开在第二层者，两边为住宿之处，正中为厅，后面则为炊爨之地也。

羌屋之平顶，为屋宇中最密之处，后面之墙，高起七八尺，上供白石神位。其一旁为矮平屋，高仅及人，以储农具及收获之食粮。屋顶后高前低，向前略斜形而偏于一角，雨水乃由最低处之木涧或石涧流出。周围（前、左、右）之墙高出屋顶约尺余，上覆以石板，以作护墙之用。屋顶之建筑，其下为口径四五寸之树木，平铺之，令彼此相接，再上铺小树枝、荆棘、竹杪等，最上铺以黏土，筑之令坚实。初建之时，遇大雨则漏，但每下雨一次，即修补一次。人在上面工作，愈久则践踏坚密，遇雨则不漏矣。但仍需时时填补，不然多次大雨之后，其上之黏土，大半将为冲刷以去也。再者羌区中之雨降之大且久，故土顶尚可支持也。

室内之陈设，均甚简单，其受汉化程度较深者，室内陈设多与汉人相同，椅、桌、板凳、床等均备，其他锅碗筷、陶器等均系由汉地运往。其物质生活，多半已汉化（调查时，需将室内所有之陈设，开一清单）。羌人室中，有一特别设备，即铁三足是也。其直径约三尺余，高二尺余，重百余斤。此三足多置于堂屋正中照壁之后，为室内生活之中心，为火炉为炊食物之所，亦为饮食之处。

三足之分布，除羌人外，西番藏人，罗罗中均用之。三足在西番藏人罗罗中，为极尊敬之物，家人及外来之客人在其前不能有不敬之举动，如烘火时将足踏其上等，羌人中现虽无此种禁忌，想当初时亦有之。如现在羌中以此三足代表火神，如家中无铁三足，必置三石以代表之。大概原来之三脚为石，铁乃后来之代替品也。

（二）农业

羌民为农业民族，故农作为其主要工作。其主要农作品为芋麦，荞子次之，青稞及麦又次之。芋麦四月种，八九月收获。此为其主要食粮，每家之中，倘能收芋麦十余石，一年生活，即可解决。芋麦之传入羌中，约在清乾隆以后。不过羌人皆以为其自祖辈以来均有之。可见民族记忆力之不可靠。其历来之主要农作，大概为麦。《后汉书》"惟以麦为资"是也。青稞为大麦之一种，其名始见于《北史》，何时传入羌中，或为其地原有之变种，则不得而知。麦及青稞，今年十月种，明年六七月收，需时甚久，非宦庶之家，不能种植。麦曲为敬客之上品，青稞则为制酒用，种法与麦同。荞子不知始于何时，为穷人之主要食品，一年可两熟，如将早芊麦收后，尚可种荞麦一季也。

羌人之农作物，除以上者外，尚有麻与烟叶。麻为其所织麻布之原料，每家必种之。《后汉书》言："不生谷、粟、麻、菽。"此语实不尽然。不生谷米则有之，至于粟、麻、菽，则盛产之也。烟则全为自吃之用。烟之传入羌中，至早亦不过在清初之际，因烟草明末始传入中国也。粟菽等类，均可种植，但羌人种之者少。蔬菜除辣椒外，亦不种。间有种小白菜秧者。其主要副产为花椒，为羌人之Cash——Crop，每担可售价五十余元。

羌人中有一种特别种植方法，彼等称之曰火地。其法将半山中坡度较平，灌木丛生之地，于夏秋之际，纵火焚之，不耕不锄，亦不施肥料（火焚后之灰，亦为一种肥料），将苦荞种遍撒之，至秋后收获。此亦前所言之"火种"也。秋后半山中花开似锦者，羌人大地所种之苦荞也。

羌人之农作方法及农具，亦多与汉人者不同，汉人农人至其地者，亦多袭用羌人之方法。羌人农具中最特别者，则为耕犁，此犁以双牛挽之：一人牵牛，一人扶犁，遇有岩石处，则提犁以避之，过石则仍插入土中。其样式较汉犁为大。颇近似古代埃及近东等处所用之犁。

（三）手工业

羌人中之手工业，极为幼稚。所有之木工金工等，均为汉人入内为之。其地之各种用具，多系购自市上，或由汉商小贩输入。他如棉布、油、盐等，均系由外面运入者。羌人惟一之手工业，则为织麻布。麻四五月种，九十月割，割后晒于屋顶，俟雨水日光浸透后，将麻皮剥下捶洗。在冬季女子无事，则打麻线，以作织麻布之用。打麻线不用纺车，而用纺锤，布织成后，必用杵在柱上捣之，制成衣后，每洗必需捶，不然者则不轻不暖。羌寨之中，早晚必闻砧杵之声，实有"住人理寒服，万结砧杵劳"之情况也。

（四）副业

背夫，为羌人男子挣钱之惟一途径，多于阴历十月后四月前，农暇之时为之。羌人不能挑抬，只能背，亦习惯使然也。又羌人不解经商，其地之商业，均由汉人为之，往其地者，安岳、乐至人为最多，即其中之土司式微，亦不知经商，如陇木司何九皋，今背于途如齐民也。羌人中之优秀儿童不令之读书，则令之学端公，亦一副业也。

羌人中最重要之副业，则为牧畜，因其地山多田少，旷地甚多，最宜于此种副业故也。牧畜以羊为主要之牲口，牛豕与马则甚少。羊则山羊绵羊均有，但以山羊为最多。山羊在羌民之信仰中，极为重要。如祭礼之牺牲，只能用山羊，不得用绵羊也。每家之羊群，穷者数十头，富者数百头。牛则多耕作之用，间亦有用马者。

羌人虽有牛群及羊群，但彼等从不用乳及乳所制之食品。亦属可怪之事。今人多以羌人原为游牧民族，此说须重加考虑。因未有曾为牧畜民族，而轻易放弃其饮乳及食乳制品之习惯也。

（五）衣饰

羌人之衣饰，有一种特别习俗，即其色尚白。彼等以白为上色，他色次之，黑色最下。如《明史》卷三一一《四川土司传》载："正德二年，太监罗鈵奏，茂州所辖卜南村、曲山等寨，乞为白人，愿纳粮差。其俗以白为善，以黑为恶。礼部覆，番人向化，宜令入贡给赏。从之。"可知其尚白，由来已久。故现在羌人中之服色，多用各质料之本色。如麻毛等均用本来之白色，而不加色素，亦崇其原来尚白之遗意也。

羌人内衣，现在几全用棉质土布，质料愈粗愈佳，至于洋布则非其所喜也。内衣制法，与汉人同，或为羌妇自制，或为汉人裁缝入内为之代制。外衣则为麻制，极粗厚耐用。衽在右，纽扣或为麻制，或竟以带代之。衣长及膝下，腰系带，外再着羊皮之短背心，或黑羊毛织之对襟长背心。此种长背心，长及膝，极厚重，可御雨，大概背心之用，除御寒外，多为背负之用。因背负时，背心厚硬，藉可减轻负重之摩擦力故也。女子之外衣，与男子略同。不过前短后长，因女子前面系围腰故也。

裹腿为男女所必用，长五六尺，宽二寸许，麻制或羊毛制，裹法与汉稍异。山上荆棘甚多，故需裹腿以作保护。羌人不戴帽，均裹帕子，羌人原来戴毡帽，帕子乃自汉人中传入，羌语中无帕子之名，仍以汉语帕子名之，可以概见也。明修《四川通志》曾载一有趣之故事："嘉靖中……风村一十七寨……诣军门请降……亡何，他寨若番牌大力孙子皆请归降，效风村故事……兵备使使石泉令李茂元受之。羌俗囚首无冠，茂元具汉冠，易其姓名书冠间，届日启军门，铙吹数部，枞树鼓大钲，令诸羌鱼鳞入。诸羌闻鼓钲，望见汉冠，及朱杆彩旗，乃大喜，举足跳舞，欢呼震天。乃出汉冠冠诸羌，诸羌跪起，各互视其首，踊跃东西走。既而又跪捧其冠以谢……"此可谓深知羌人心理。不过此处言羌俗囚首无冠，不知何所指也。

在清时羌人原蓄辫，现在黑水中尚如此。其他处羌人将发全行剃去，惟颅顶留发撮约钱大，长约四五寸。女子发式如汉女，挽簪，闺女则梳辫，长则盘于头之周围。女子亦裹帕。

女子之戒指手镯，均为银制，多仿汉式。现在羌中最时髦之耳环，则为一绿色之玉石，约铜元大小，中穿小孔，贯以银环。汶川、理番、茂县之羌女均如此。至黑虎寨及黑水中，则银环加大，重约两余。

其他之随身物品，最重要者，则为烟斗及铜烟盒，男女必备。幼童自十四五岁后即带之。女子必带针筒一只，上缀以穗、珠饰、铜钱等物。

六、羌人之政治组织

羌人之政治组织，历代以来，均极散漫。事急则彼此相依，事过则互相攻击，故自秦汉以来，羌民族之人数虽众，所占之地域虽广，而从未建立强大之帝国。其中虽不乏杰出之士，如前秦符氏，后秦姚氏等，但皆窃据一方，较之元人之征服欧亚，满清之入主中原，则瞠乎其后矣。推原其故，厥为缺乏组织是也。记载中之所能见者，如《后汉书》所言："不立君臣，无相长一，强则分种为酋豪，弱则为人附落，更相抄暴，以力为雄，杀人偿死，无他禁令。其兵常在山谷，短于平地，不能持久，而果于触突，以战死为吉利，病终为不祥，堪耐寒苦，同之禽兽。"自是以后，莫不如此。如《北史》所载羌之一种名宕昌者，言其"姓别自为部落，酋帅皆有地分，不相统摄"。至唐时羌种之最强者，如党项，亦复如是。《旧唐书》："其种每姓别自为部落，一姓之中，复分为小部落，大者万余骑，小者数千骑，不相统一。"此其所谓原始，不奴役于汉人，即奴役于藏人也。

唐以前之所谓酋帅，即元明之所谓土司，现在羌人土司中，亦有能溯其世系至于唐世者，不过其受中朝封爵多起自元明。故自元明而后，其世系均班斑可考。清亦沿袭明制，甚少变革。兹将清代之重要土司列于后。

汶川县：

瓦寺宣慰使司（原为乌思藏人，明万历间平羌人后，驻牧于汶川县之涂禹山）

理番县：

梭磨宣慰司

卓克基长官司

松冈长官司（以上皆羌戎西番杂居）

九子屯（清乾隆间征金川后多已戎化而尚保存羌俗）

茂县：

静州长官司

岳希长官司

陇木长官司

长宁安抚司

水草坪巡检司（土司苏朝□家藏有明万历敕文）

竹木坎副巡检司（土司孙振寅现为联保主任住椒子坪）

牟托巡检土司

实大关副长官司

大定沙坝土千户

松坎土百户

大姓土百户

小姓土百户

小姓黑水土百户

以上不过就其有后裔及衙署可寻者。清代之增减损益尚不止此也。按：土司不一定为羌人，亦有有功汉人，效庄蹻之王滇者。亦有藏人因征剿羌人，而遂长其地者。如瓦寺土司，原为乌斯藏人，明万历中，因征羌人而驻牧其地。其中尚有原带来之一部藏人，至今尚保存其一部分之语言。

现在土司制虽已取消，大半之土司，均已衰落，而尚有一部分之土司，虽无其位，尚有莫大之潜在势力。其一举一动，均为羌人所畏服。其编有保甲之区，土司多为联保主任，县政府亦无如之何。是亦土司之变相也。

羌人性爱自由，尚平等，崇独立，为极端之个人主义，此其所以无大规模之政治组织，及明清以来，时常反抗土司制之由来也。因应付流官易，流官之任期亦有限，而土司之剥削，则终身无所逃避故也。土司制为酋长制之变相，但土司制之功能及其实施之方式，至今尚未有能知其详者。

七、羌人之社会组织

《西羌传》言："其俗氏族无定，或以父名母姓为种号，十二世后，相与婚姻。"《冉駹夷传》亦言"贵妇人，党母族"。故有根据此言，以为羌人原系母系社会，《后汉书》所言为母系社会之遗留。彼等又列举羌人中"上门"之风盛行，入赘则女子不出母家，亦可认为母系组织之遗。其羌人亡后，无论男女，必通知母族，若系女子，除通知母族（彼等名曰母舅）外，亦须通知母族之母族（羌人称曰母舅），彼等至时，则举止傲慢，丧家对之，则极尽恭敬之能事。论者亦认为此种风俗为母系之遗。

不过此种解释于理论上颇有困难。因前者曾以羌人为游牧民族，而游牧民族中，则甚少有母系社会者。故吾人若以羌人原为母系社会，则不当言其为游牧民族矣。《后汉书》中所言，其词颇为恍惚，不能知其真意所在。如氏族无定，与贵妇人党母族等，并不一定为母系社会之遗留也。

羌人中现在之氏族，则全无组织，但从其文化之他方面观之，尚可见其氏族制度之痕迹。如同姓不婚（当以羌姓为准，汉姓不足据），或为宗族外婚制之遗。《西羌传》"十二世后，相与婚姻"之言，实不足为典据。十二代所经之时间，至少需二三百年，但经如许久之时间后，又谁复能记忆之者。又普通之原始民族中之同族可通婚者，仅三世或五世后即可，不然者，虽百世亦不可也。据余所知，羌人中姨表姊妹可以为婚，而姑表姊妹，则不能为婚：询其意则云，姑与父相似之处太多，而姨母则不然。果如此，则原为母系民族之问题，亦不能成立。从前羌人火葬时，同族之人，均须到场，母姓则否。在每年十月初一还愿之时，如一寨中有数姓居人，则每一姓备羊一头，由端公祭山神后，每姓各人将羊携至家分食。在此时用羊膊骨所向之吉凶，亦各以每一姓为分界。

羌人之火坟，亦每姓一座，绝不相混。不过现在因采用穴葬，此习已废，然可见其为宗族组织之遗也。

羌人中财产与姓氏之遗传，均从父传子，女子除嫁奁外，别无其他权利。即如端公，亦多父子相承，其法器亦传子而不传徒。

羌人中之工作及活动之中心，以一寨为单位，而不以宗族为单位。每一寨之中，少则一二姓，多则四五姓，而少有一姓一寨者。凡一切经济活动，社会仪式，均全寨人赴之，而不以一族为一族之单独举动也。如其宗教大典，四月初一之开山，十月初一之还愿，均以一寨同雇一端公行之，而不一姓为一姓之还愿也。其神林及山神，均为一寨所公有，而一寨又有一寨之公山，为该寨樵苏之所。他寨之人，不得侵犯。如农作忙时，则寨中人互相帮助，不以宗族而分轩轾也。

每寨之中，并无一定之正式首领，不过有一二人为众人公认之领袖，此种领导人物，并非世袭，亦非以家资富有而定，乃全以个人之才能而定。此类人平常为寨中人所信服，遇有纠纷时，则皆取决之。现在凡编有保甲之区，政府多以之为保甲长。

八、婚姻

据典籍所载，羌人之婚俗，多与西北民族相同。《后汉书》："父没则妻后母，兄亡则纳釐嫂，故国无鳏寡，种类繁殖。"又如《北史·宕昌羌传》："父子伯叔兄弟死者，即以继母、世叔母及嫂弟妇等为妻。"再如《旧唐书·党项羌传》："妻其庶母及伯叔母嫂子弟之妇，谣秽蒸亵，诸夷中最为甚，然不婚同姓。"其他之例尚多，今不过略举一二，以明自汉以至唐宋，其婚俗莫不如此。此种收继婚，为西北游牧民族之特征，因其文化之背景及环境之需要，不得不如此也。但又可为羌人为非母系民族之旁证。

　　整理者说明：此系根据今存之油印稿整理写定，稿纸每页版心皆刻印有"西南民族史"字样，知其为计划中系统专著《西南民族史》之部分内容。成稿时间估计在20世纪40年代中。

张勋燎

　　（原载四川大学历史文化学院考古学系编：《四川大学考古专业创建四十周年暨冯汉骥教授百年诞辰纪念文集》，四川大学出版社，2001年，第26—37页）

民族学与边政

赵瓯北为镇安知府时，以其民风淳朴，政简刑轻，大有终身安之，不复思迁之概。但对于边民的的礼俗，却闹了一个笑柄。他所着的《檐曝杂记》①（卷三）中，于边境风俗曾记载一段说："粤西土民，及滇黔苗□，风俗大概皆淳朴，惟男女之事，不甚有别……其视野田草露之事，不过如内地人看戏赌钱之类，非异事也。……凡男女私相结，谓之拜同年，又谓之做后生，多在未婚娶以前。谓嫁娶生子，则须作合成家，不复可为此游戏。是以其俗成婚虽早，然初婚时，夫妻例不同宿。婚夕其女即拜一邻姬为干娘，与之同寝，三日内为翁姑挑水数担，即归母家。其后虽亦时至夫家，仍不同寝，恐生子不能做后生也。大抵念四五岁以前，皆系做后生之时，女既出拜男同年，男亦拜女同年。至念四五以后，嬉游之性已退，愿成家室，于是

_____

① 原文无书名号，书名号系整理者所加。

夫妻始同处。以故恩意多不笃，偶因反目，辄至离异，皆由于少年不即成婚之故也。余在镇安时，欲革此俗，下令凡婚者不许异寝，镇民闻之皆笑，以为此事非太守所当与闻也。"

这一段记载，大半是很正确的。在苗瑶社会中，做后生与拜同年，为女子一生中最自由、最甜蜜、最宝贵的时期，为青年所应享的幸福，任何人都不能加以干涉的。瓯北先生想用一纸告示，革除此根深蒂固的风俗，当然要为苗瑶所笑，以堂堂朝廷官吏，干涉人民的房第之私了。不过瓯北终是史学家，能自己记录下来，想抱着"用夏变夷"思想的边疆官吏中，这类的笑柄，决不只此，不过不能像瓯北一样的坦率罢了！例如清时李来章为广西连阳令时，曾想革除苗瑶的歌舞，出示禁止，不祇不发生效力，而其歌舞也愈甚，有人作竹枝词笑他说："红粉平看一任人，江干分外有阳春！兰乡太守真多事，示禁花歌浪费神。"

兰乡为李来章之字，照我们看来，兰乡太守不只"多事"，若严厉的执行起来，恐怕要"偾事"了！因为在以前许多边民的叛变，并不是完全由于官吏之压迫剥削和边民之好乱，而好多是由于汉人的官吏，过于违反了他们的习俗，边人在忍无可忍之下，只有起而反抗了。

赵翼和李来章的态度，可以说，能代表历来一般汉官对于边民礼俗的态度，我们看他们所留下来的记载中，总是说：下车之始，即禁示××，一套的堂皇文章。然而他又何尝禁得住。但现在则不同了，例如：近来有许多作边疆行政工作的朋友，往往与作者谈到这一些问题，都以为欲顺利的推行边政，非加以研究及改变观念不可，并不是将我们汉人的这一套，搬到边疆去，就行得通的！我们必须另寻妥善的办法，在民族学中找出路。

民族学为研究文化的科学，在初本为一纯理科学，并未有想用以来解决实际问题的。不过民族学也与其他的纯理科学一样，不能永远地离开实际人生，不闻不问，孤独研究。故一待其理论成熟，终须应用至文化之实际上问题的。如民族学所研究的，为民族及文化的接触、传播、吸收、同化、分合、整化诸等等问题，由之成立原则，以期能预知文化之发展方向，而终之加以控制。然而此亦是边疆行政上的问题，因为边政上的主要问题，至少自理论上讲，为一民族接触及文化融合问题。因为两个文化或民族要和平相处，不拘是一方面的统治，或是相互的善意提携，均必须先互相了解而共谋融合之道，方为有效。此在欧美国家内之包含多种不同民族或多殖民族之国家中，近数十年来应用民族学的知识来解决民族间关系问题的事实上看来，即是很显明的。

不过还有少数民族学家，以为民族学之此种应用，是很危险的，因为倘若如此，不只民族学要失掉其理论独立性，或将变为政治的附庸。而知识也是极危险的东西，用之不得其当，危害亦是很大的。倘如民族学对于某某民族的知识，落在野心政治家的手里，利用它来无形中消灭一种民族，是极容易的事。这当然是因噎废食的见解，我们不能因为自然科学为野心家应用来作杀人的利器，就想停止自然科学的研究与应用，一样是不必要的。

再者，在另一方面，有若干边疆行政家，以为民族学家的理论，是纸上空谈，书生之见，用之不只无济于事，反而要增加行政上许多麻烦，不如完全不知道的好。这种见解，当然亦是不正确的。他们要开发边疆的资源，他们知道利用地质学、矿物学、地理学及经济学上的知识。难道治理边疆民族，就不能利用民族学上研究所得的知识吗？这是可以不言而喻的。

民族学与边政学的结合，是必然的趋势。因为一种科学的研究，到了某种程度，必须顾到应用的问题，而不能与实际生活脱节。而实际问题发生欲求解决时，亦不能置科学的研究的发现于不顾，自甘于暗中摸索。

现在如英国、荷兰等之多殖民地的国家，对于派往殖民地负责直接行政责任的官吏，往往先施以民族学的训练，各大学中设有此有此类专科，各地设有民族关系研究所或实验室，专事研究文化同化的问题。又各殖民地又多派有民族学专家作顾问，遇有困难发生时，可备行政官吏的咨询，或研究解决的方案。行之十余年，颇着成效，不祇可以增加行政上的效率，避免无谓的浪费，而且可以避免许多不幸冲突的发生。

又如在此次大战中，美国对于民族学知识的应用，可以说，是史无前例的。战争中在这次，美军几在全球作战，在太平洋，在亚洲，在菲洲，都有美军的战场。开拔往各战场军队中的军官，均授以该地的民族学的知识。而随军亦各派有民族学专家，随时指导，以避免军队与土人间的摩擦，及博得土人的合作。另一方面教授士兵以该地民族生活方式及利用环境的方法，借以增强作战能力及生存机会。

这在作战之中，可以说是别开生面的。

　　我们有广大的边疆，其间有众多的民族。这些民族，都曾与我们有深长的历史关系和密切的接触，种族亦都相同。我们要开发边疆，必须先要提携其间的民族，不然，资源是把握不住的。外蒙、新疆之倾向苏联，西藏之倾向英国，未必是完全由于武力的压迫，或其他的诱惑，而我们不能了解他们，恐怕还是主要原因。在我们境内，所有的民族是一律平等，这早就昭示在各族之间，我们若以稍微先进者自居，我们有提携他们的义务，俾能共达康乐之境。欧西等国家对于殖民地民族采取剥削榨取政策者，尚知应用民族学的知识以治理之，而况我们为边民谋幸福而不利用科学乎？所以我们以后的边政，必须建立在民族学的基础之上。

（原载《西方日报》1947 年 11 月 28 日第四版

《中国边疆》副刊第一期）

由中国亲属名词上所见之中国古代婚姻制

　　近来研究中国古代社会进化者，莫不以摩尔根（L.H.Morgan）之社会进化阶段为其立论根据。但摩尔根之社会进化思想，特其表现于《古代社会》一书之中者，多与近来新发现之事实不合，故现在研究人类之社会进化者，即根本否认普遍之社会的进化有同一固定之程序，有如摩尔根及其他十九世纪中诸社会进化论者所主张者。不过从学术之发展上视之，摩尔根之所以为十九世纪伟大社会学家之一者，并不在其社会进化阶段之划分，而在其发现亲属名词与社会制度之关系；并不在其《古代社会》一书，而在《人类中之血族与姻族之系统》一书。[①]不过后者之篇帙繁重，措词专门，不为学者所习知耳。

　　《人类中之血族与姻族之系统》一书，出版于1871年，当是时麦

---

① *Systems of Consanguinity and Affinity of the Human Family*. 1871.摩尔根氏在此书中收集世界各民族之亲属名词，而加以分析。其性质固瑕瑜互见。但其收集之数量则至为可惊。其《古代社会》中之社会进化理论，即根据于此书之所得。世人只知其《古代社会》而不知有此书，固莫由窥摩尔根学说之真谛也。

克令南曾力加以反驳，^①彼以为亲属名词与社会组织无甚重大关系，不过为一种"称呼词"而已。但平心论之，摩尔根之论证可议之处固甚多，究不失为社会学上一极重大之发现。麦克令南系一业律师出身之社会学家，长于辩才，其对于摩尔根之攻击，每多过分之处。故一般学者，多左麦克令南而右摩尔根。自是之后，摩尔根所谓之"类分式的（classificatory）"亲属制，及"叙述式的（descriptive）"亲属制遂成社会学中之口头术语矣。

但亲属制度研究上之争论，并不自此而终止。如克洛伯于1909年在其最著名之《类分式的亲属制》一文中，^②又旧事重提，以为亲属名词，不过为一种语言上及心理上之现象，与社会组织，无任何关系。克洛伯并详论亲属制之分为"类分式的"及"叙述式的"之不当。因摩尔根所认为"叙述式的"亲属制中，亦有"类分式"之名词，而"类分式"的亲属制中，亦有"叙述式"之名词也。自克洛伯此文发表之后，瑞弗斯乃根据其在海洋洲所得之亲属制度资料，对克洛伯加以反驳。^③瑞弗斯以为摩尔根之推论，诚多有错误，但彼为此问题研究之开始者，筚路蓝缕，其开创之功，自不可没，况其在大端上，尚不失为极重要之发现乎？吾人自不能因其小疵而弃其大醇也。瑞弗斯所著之《亲属与社会组织》一书，为其精心之作，论亲属制度

---

① J. F. Mclennan, *Studies in Ancient History*. 1876.摩尔根在其《古代社会》附录中有所答辩，可参见杨东莼、张栗原译本，925—961面。杨张二氏之汉译，竟将书名译错，可知其未见麦克令南之原书也。

② A. L. Kroeber, Classificatory Systems of Relationship, *Journal, Journal of the Royal Anthropological Institute*. 1909, 39: 77–84. 克洛伯此文之真贡献，并非在其批评"类分式的"一名词之不当，而在其亲属名词中categories之鉴定，为后来之研究亲属制度者另创一新工具。

③ W.H.R.Rivers, *Kinship and Social Organization*（《亲属与社会组织》）1914.

之书中，现在尚无出其右者。瑞弗斯在此书中畅论亲属名词与婚姻制度之关系，于"交表婚姻制"论列尤详，为后来之研究婚姻制度者，辟一新途径。

论中国亲属称谓与婚姻之关系者，在欧西则有格兰内、[1]施爱客[2]等，但皆偶一及之，词意闪烁，未能得其详也。国人著述中亦稍稍有及之者，如郭沫若之《中国古代社会研究》及陈顾远之《中国婚姻史》中，均以"诸父"、"诸母"、"兄弟"、"亚壻"、"娣姒"等称，以推论古代"群婚"之制。然皆囿于见闻，绌于方法，不能脱出摩尔根之圈套。[3]再者，"群婚"之俗，是否真有其事，亦为现在之人类学者所否认。

婚姻制度之最能与亲属名词发生关系者，莫过于交表婚、姊妹同婚及收继婚三种。人类学者于研究亲属名词之特征时，或推衍特种婚姻制度之实在性与普遍性时，往往将二者互为利用，交相解释。因亲属名词之形式为语言现象，而语言为事实之表征。又语言之变演，每较其所表现之事实为缓。往往一事物早归淘汰，然其表现于语言名

① M. Granet, *La civilization chinois*, 1929. 此书之引证事实，可谓亟牵强附会之能事，然彼亦自有其立场也。

② J. K. Shryock and T. S. Chen: Chinese Relationship Terms, *American Anthropologist*, 34:4, 623–669，其他如Ⅱ. p. Wilkinson之The Chinese Family Nomenclature, *New China Review* (1921), 159–191，则更卑卑不足道矣。

③ 摩尔根之学说，已成为学术史上之陈迹，其在现在学术上之地位，可参考B. J. Stern, *Lewis Henry Morgan, Social Evolutionist*. 1931. 当摩尔根之著作发表之初，即为马克思及恩格斯所采用，故后之崇共产主义者，因欲尊马克思，故亦奉摩尔根之《古代社会》为天经地义，莫之或易。彼等固不得不如此者，因若否认摩尔根之说，即否认马克思学说之根据也。郭沫若之《中国古代社会研究》一书，并非能以实事求是之精神以研究中国古代社会者，不过欲借中国之资料，以证明古代之原始共产社会而已。其盲从主义，昧于学术之进展，自属幼稚，然彼亦自有其立场也。若陈顾远之《中国婚姻史》，亦拾摩尔根、郭沫若之馀唾，可谓不知所从矣。

词上者，独立存在，或稍变其义以名其他后起或相类似之事物。故研究古代制度者，时时利用语言之现象，以推求古代之事物，所谓"语言的古生物学（linguistic paleontology）"，盖实有其事也。

交表婚姻制

何谓交表亲属（cross-cousin）？"交表亲属"为人类学上研究亲属制度之术语，其意义仍系对平表亲属（parallel-cousin）而言，[①]姑母之子女，舅父之子女，与己身（ego）为交表亲属，因姑母与父为异性，而舅父与母亦为异性也。伯叔父之子女，及姨母之子女，与己身为平表亲属，因伯叔父与父为同性，而姨母与母亦为同性也。但交表亲属与平表亲属在婚姻上之意义，并不由于其亲属"所自来"性别上之分，而在其在于宗族制度中亲属分配之不同。如在母系制度之下，姨母之子女与己身同属于一宗族之内，在宗族外婚制之下，故不能互为婚姻。在父系制度中，父之兄弟之子女，与己身属于同一宗族之内，在宗族外婚制之下，亦不得互为婚姻。舅父之子女，与姑母之子女，不拘其系在父系或母系制度之下，均与己身所属之宗族不同，故不受外婚制之影响，而可互为婚姻。

交表婚姻，又分二种。在若干原始民族中，有只能与舅父之子女

---

① "交表"亦有作中表者。但俗所谓"中表"之涵义，亦有将姨母之子包括在内者，与人类学上所用之cross-cousin不合，故不用。

为婚，而不能与姑母之子女为婚者；又有只能与姑母之子女为婚，而不能与舅父之子女为婚者。此种婚俗，称之曰"单系的"交表婚。再在许多民族中，舅父之子女及姑母之子女，与己身均可互为婚姻，此种制度，称之曰"双系的"交表婚。

在人类学上之所谓交表婚姻，并非如现行之所谓"中表婚"，其执行为两造父母或本人之自由意志而定。此处之所谓交表婚姻者，乃系一种有"优先权的（preferential）"、"指定性的"或"强迫性的"婚制。例如本身为男子，而姑母有女，本身至少与姑母之女有结婚之优先权。若姑母之女欲与他人结婚者，至少须得本身之许可，或须给相当之补偿，甚至非与之结婚不可。如《贵州通志》所言清江黑苗之婚嫁风俗："姑之女定为舅媳，倘舅无子，必献重金于舅，谓之外甥钱，否则终身不得嫁。"

汉族在古时有无此种"指定的"交表婚姻，载籍之中，未曾明言，其曾存在与否，须由他方证验之推断。在推论之先，可先论交表婚姻在我国现在之情形如何。

所谓交表婚姻，记载中之实例，自周秦以来，不胜枚举。现在各地之风俗中，亦多有行之者。不过在理论上则为所不许，在法律上，亦为所禁止。如《白虎通》卷一〇：

> 外属小功以上，亦不得娶也。是以春秋传曰，讥娶母党也。[1]

---

[1] 此篇所引之卷数，为淮南书局刻陈立《白虎通·疏证》本。

又《通典》（卷六〇）引晋袁准内表不可为婚议：

> 曰：今之人内外相婚礼钦？曰：中外之亲，近于同姓，同姓且犹不可，而况中外之亲乎！古人以为无疑，故不制也。今以古之不言，因谓之可婚，此不知礼者也。

袁准此论，引申过甚，不免有曲解之嫌。细考言礼者之所以反对交表婚姻者，并非由其血统之太近，而实由于其不合乎礼。其不合乎礼之处，即为双重亲属在丧服上所发生之纠纷是也。何以言之？例如姑之女与己之兄结婚，倘其亡故时，以叔嫂论则无服，以表姊弟论则有服。此问题在唐以前之论礼著作中，讨论綦多，又均各执己见，不肯相下。故最简便之解决方法，莫若以此种婚姻为根本不合乎礼，则服制问题，当然不解决而自行解决矣。

在法律上之禁止，说者以为始于唐律，如《唐律疏议·户婚》：

> 其父母之姑舅两姨姊妹，……并不得为婚……

洪迈《容斋续笔》卷八，曾记在宋时即有据此文以禁止中表为婚者，其言曰：

> 姑舅兄弟为婚，在礼法不禁，而世俗不晓。案刑统户婚律

云：① 父母之姑舅两姨姊妹，及姨，若堂姨；母之姑，堂姑；己之堂姨，及再从姨，堂外甥女，女婿姊妹，并不得为婚。议曰：父母姑舅两姨姊妹，于身无服，乃是父母缌麻，据身是尊，故不合娶。及姨又是父母大功尊，若堂姨虽于父母无服，亦是尊属。母之姑，堂姑，并是母小功以上尊。己之堂姨，及再从姨，堂外甥女，亦谓堂姊妹所生者，女婿姊妹，于身虽并无服，据理不可为婚。并为尊卑混乱，人伦失序之故。然则中表兄弟姊妹，正是一等，其于婚姻，了无所妨……今州县官书判至有将姑舅兄弟成婚而断离之者，皆失于不能细读律令也。

洪氏所言良是，唐律所禁者，（《宋刑统》此条乃全据《唐律疏议》之文）为尊卑（即不同辈分者）为婚，而非中表为婚也。不过洪氏言为"礼法所不禁"，似未深考，法虽不禁，而在礼则所不许也。②

律例中之明文禁止中表为婚姻者，则为明律。《明律集解·户婚》：

若娶己之姑舅两姨姊妹者，杖八十，并离异。

清律全袭其文，不过法律自法律，风俗自风俗，若尽执法以

---

① 《刑统》系谓《宋刑统》。此律文系全袭《唐律疏议》。

② 如《通典》卷九五："大唐之制，两姨姑舅姊妹并不得通婚。"此乃据礼言之，而非据律言之也。至于西魏文帝时禁中外及从母兄弟姊妹为婚，周武帝曾下诏不得娶母同姓以为妻妾，宣帝又诏母族绝服外者听婚等等，皆系外族之婚制，又当别论也。

绳，则杖不胜杖，离不胜离矣。故《清律例》在此律文后，《条例》中则言："其姑舅两姨姊妹为婚者，听从民便。"

中国历来法律之矛盾，大抵如是。

交表婚姻，在现在中国之社会中，为一种矛盾的现象，一方面为礼法所不许，而民间行之者甚多。但在古代，交表婚姻，不只为礼法所许，而为一种"强制的"婚俗，此种现象，在中国古代之亲属名词上，即可见之。

记载古代亲属名词之最完备者，当推《尔雅·释亲》及《仪礼·丧服传》。二书之时代，以其所载之亲属名词推之，《释亲》当较早，《丧服传》较晚，但均不得晚于西汉。换言之，即公元以前之物也。作亲属名词上之推论者，若能知其时代之大概，即已足用，因亲属名词之变演，为时甚缓，非一朝一夕之可能就，常需经过数十年或数百年之间也。本篇所引之亲属名词，多以《尔雅》为主，再挽以他书，而用《丧服传》以补其不足。

《尔雅·释亲》（《丧服传》同）所载之亲属名词，有数种特征，与现行之亲属名词不同，历来之说经者，均陈陈相因，不得其解。如《释亲》：

母之晜弟为舅。

妇称夫之父曰舅。

妻之父为外舅。

父之姊妹为姑。

　　　　夫之母为姑。
　　　　妻之母为外姑。

　　是"舅"之一名词，包括母之兄弟、夫之父及妻之父。"姑"则包括母之姊妹、夫之母及妻之母。如此复杂之亲属关系，而以两名词统括之，自非偶然，其中必有重大之原因在也。解经者之说，如《白虎通》：

　　　　称夫之父母为舅姑何？尊如父而非父者，舅也。亲如母而非母者，姑也。故称夫之父母为舅姑也。

又如《释名》：

　　　　妻之父曰外舅，母曰外姑，言妻从外来，谓至己家为归，故反此义以称之，夫妇匹敌之义也。

　　以上之解释，读之仍令人茫然。如"尊如父而非父者"，何必为舅？伯叔父岂不是一样？"亲如母而非母者"，何必曰姑？姨母岂不较姑更为亲似？至于《释名》，则只解释"外"字，而并未解释"舅"与"姑"字也，[1]然舅姑二名词所含之意义，从交表婚姻制观

---

① 陈顾远《中国婚姻史》，八七面及二〇七面，以为舅姑之义，为交换婚之遗，真不自知其所云为何也。

之，则甚为明瞭，不必作种种之臆测也。

如己身（女）与母之昆弟之子结婚，则母之昆弟（舅）与夫之父为一人，以"舅"一名词统之，固属自然。再如己身（女）与父之姊妹之子结婚，则父之姊妹（姑）与夫之母又为一人，以"姑"一名词统之，亦属自然也。吾人当知，在亲属关系增加之程序上，舅（母之昆弟）姑（父之姊妹）之关系在先，舅（夫之父）姑（夫之母）之关系在后，以先有之名词，加诸后来增加之关系上，在语言上固属自然之趋势也。

反之，己身（男）若与母之昆弟之女结婚，则母之昆弟（舅）与妻之父为一人。又如己身（男）与父之姊妹之女结婚，则父之姊妹（姑）与妻之母同为一人。以同上之理由，舅姑之名，亦可加之于妻之父母也。

舅姑二名词所表现者，为"双系的"交表婚姻制，即己身能与舅姑之子女互为婚姻是也。但《尔雅》所载亲属名词之特征，并不只此，又如，《释亲·妻党》：

　　姑之子为甥，舅之子为甥，妻之昆弟为甥，姊妹之夫为甥。

以"甥"之一名词，统括四种不同之亲属，最为奇特。历来之解经者，均以郭注为主：

　　四人体敌，故更相为甥。甥，犹生也。

"体敌"为相等之义，但如何为"体敌"？从未有人能作明白之解释者。如俞樾之"姑之子为甥，舅之子为甥，妻之昆弟为甥，姊妹之夫为甥解"，[①]洋洋数百言，仍不能说出体敌之义何在也。如姑舅之子体敌，而从母（姨母）之子如何不能敌体？再者妻之昆弟为姻族亲属（affinal relatives），姑舅之子为血族亲属（consanguineal relatives），其性质迥然不同，而彼此何能"敌体"？诸如此类，皆必须明白之解释者也。

《释名》曾将"妻之昆弟为甥"加以解释云：

> 妻之昆弟曰外甥，其姊妹女也，来归己内为妻，故其男为外姓之甥。甥者，生也。他姓子本生于外，不得如其女来在己内也。

此乃望文生义之臆说，不足为据。然则，"甥"一名词将作何诠释乎？曰，此亦交表婚姻及姊妹交换婚（sister exchange）之表现也。何以言之？

若己身（男）与姑之女结婚，则姑之子与妻之昆弟同为一人。又如己身（男）与舅之女为婚，则舅之子与妻之昆弟，又同为一人。在双系的交表婚姻制之下，己身若不与舅之女为婚，即与姑之女为婚。故姑之子，舅之子，妻之昆弟，实际上实属相等，故可以一名词统之也。又若在双系的交表婚姻制之下，姑之子，或舅之子，娶己身之姊妹为妻（彼等均系交表亲属，故可为婚。如是则为互相交换姊

---

① 见《诂经精舍自课文》，春在堂全书本。

妹为妻矣），则己身姊妹之夫，与姑之子，舅之子，妻之昆弟亦属相等，故皆可以"甥"名之也。

如此，则历来经师所不能明者，可以一旦冰释。而同时"甥"之义，与"姑"、"舅"之义相辅而行，均为交表婚姻制之表现。又交换姊妹为婚，常与交表婚姻制并行，因己身及己身之姊妹，与姑之子女，舅之子女，互为交表亲属，故可互为婚姻①，此在原始民族中为例固甚多也。

由上之亲属名词观之，双系的交表婚在中国古代之存在，可无疑义。但何以知其为一种"强制性"的婚俗？此亦至易明瞭。如婚姻可以自由选择，则舅之子不一定娶姑之女，而姑之女亦不一定为舅之媳。若此则《尔雅》中所言"姑"、"舅"、"甥"之义与亲属之实际不合，则无由发生矣。换言之，婚俗当有多少之"强制性"始能影响到亲属名词也。

姊妹同婚

姊妹同婚（sororate）者，为姊妹同嫁一夫之谓。然其方式，亦稍有不同。例如己身娶一女子为妻，则妻之姊妹，亦得有娶之之权利。如妻之姊妹欲另嫁时，须得己身之许可，或给相当之赎偿。再者

---

① 经籍中每以"婚媾"二字并用。据许氏《说文》：媾，重婚也。段注："重婚者，重叠交互为婚也。"是"媾"之一词，似与将姊妹互相交换为之婚俗上，亦不无关系也。

如妻不育或亡故时，妻族须另备一女子，以补妻之缺。此女子必为妻之姊妹，如无姊妹，妻之兄弟之女（即内侄女）亦可。后者称为"内侄女婚"，为姊妹同婚之引申。因妻之兄弟之女，为妻之姊妹最好之代替人也。原始民族中多有行此种婚俗者，如北美印第安人中之Miwok及Omaha族，即其例也。

　　姊妹同婚，在周时颇为盛行，而特以统治阶级为尤甚[1]。古代亲属名词中，亦稍有具此俗之表征者，如《尔雅·释亲》："女子谓姊妹之夫为私。"又《诗·硕人》："谭公维私。"传统的诠释，如《释名》所言："姊妹互相谓夫为私，言于其夫兄弟中，此人与己姊妹有恩私也。"此说亦稍觉牵强。果如是，则男子亦可称姊妹之夫为私，何以"私"之名词，只限于女子间之互称也。与其间接的言于己之姊妹有恩私，不如直接的释为与己有恩私也。如是则"私"当为姊妹同婚之表现。不过此种推论，尚欠明瞭。《尔雅》又谓："母之姊妹为从母。"从母之义，以其为从母而来，以作父妾，后虽不来，亦得以从母呼之也[2]。如此义，则"从母"之名，亦当为姊妹同婚之遗也。不过"从母"亦可谓为"从父"之对称[3]，不必一定为姊妹同婚之表现。

　　在周时贵族中盛行一种姊妹同婚及内侄女婚，经传中称之曰媵。《公羊传》庄公十九年：

---

[1]　可参见 M. Granet, *La polygynie sororale et le sororat dans la Chine féodale*, 1920. 格兰内之解说，多不可凭信，不过其收集之材料，尚为丰富。

[2]　《释名·释亲属》："母之姊妹……礼谓之从母，为娣而来，则从母列也。"故虽不来，犹以此名之也。

[3]　《尔雅义疏》："从母者，犹宗族中之有从父，言从母而得尊称也。"

　　媵者何？诸侯娶一国，二国往媵之，以侄娣从。侄者何？
兄之子也。娣者何？弟也。

　　媵婚之制，共为九女，所谓"诸侯一聘九女"是也。此九女共
分三组，一为诸侯所聘之正妻（夫人），及其一侄一娣。再为二国来
伴嫁之媵，称为左媵右媵，媵各一侄一娣。共三组，合为九女。来媵
者，必与所聘之正妻同姓，《左传》成公十八年：

　　卫人来媵共姬，礼也。凡诸侯嫁女，同姓媵之，异姓则否。

　　媵妾之必为同姓者，取其可为姊妹（娣）及兄弟之女（侄），亦
即姊妹同婚及内侄女婚之遗意也。前人不察，以为无甚意义，则过
矣。但媵妾之来，在理论上不可以强求，须出自来媵者之自愿。《公
羊传》，庄公十九年，何休注：

　　言往媵之者礼，君不求媵，二国自往媵夫人，所以一夫人
之尊。

　　其用意虽为"所以一夫人之尊"，此或者出于往媵者之意，而在
于嫁女者方面，亦为不欲"求人为贱"之义。《白虎通》（卷一〇）：

　　所以不聘妾者，何？人有子孙，欲尊之，义不可求人为贱

也……妾虽贤不得为嫡。

　　媵婚制度之意义何在？当以《白虎通》所言者，为最详尽：

　　　　天子诸侯一娶九女者何？重国广继嗣也。[1]
　　　　大夫成功受封，得备八妾者，重国广嗣也。[2]
　　　　不娶两娣何？博异气也。娶三国女何？广异类也。恐一国血脉相似，以无子也。[3]
　　　　备侄娣从者，为其必不相嫉妒也。一人有子，三人共之，若己生之也。[4]

　　媵婚之制，可谓周详。而其原始姊妹同婚之痕迹，则至为明显。前已言之，在姊妹同婚制下，若妻不育时，得收妻之姊妹或侄女为妻妾，以期其有子。不过在媵婚制度之下，组织较为完密，不论妻之育与不育，诸侯大夫为"重国广嗣"计得收妻之侄娣，先备媵妾。至于"备侄娣从者"之意，"为其必不相嫉妒"，在事实上或不尽然，但亦与原始民族之有姊妹同婚制者之解释，为同一说法也。

　　此为媵婚制之大概，他如媵婚制下之"诸侯不再娶"，[5]媵妾不得

---

① 《白虎通疏证》卷一〇，页11。
② 《白虎通疏证》卷一〇，页13。
③ 《白虎通疏证》卷一〇，页11。
④ 《白虎通疏证》卷一〇，页11。又《公羊传》庄公十九年，何休注："必以侄娣从之者，欲使一人有子，二人喜也。"所以防嫉妒，令继重嗣也。因以备尊尊亲亲也。
⑤ 《公羊传》庄公十九年："诸侯一聘九女，诸侯不再娶。"

称夫人，[①]媵妾幼可以"待年父母之国"[②]等，乃为媵婚制中后起之枝节，然不能掩盖姊妹同婚之原来面目也。

关于媵婚再有一问题，即"娣"之是否为夫人或媵之同母之妹是也。毛际盛以为凡媵婚中之娣，均为媵妾之子。《说文解字述谊》卷二：

> 古不以同母妹为娣，宣姜二女一为宋桓夫人，一为许穆夫人。庄姜同母姊妹一适荆，一适谭可证也。且夫人所出，恒为夫人，娣之所出，恒为娣，所谓贵贱有常也。

毛氏之论，自有根据，不过娣之是否为夫人之亲妹，并不关重要。因在原始姊妹同婚之俗中，名词至关重要，只需有姊妹之名，不拘其为正出或庶出，均得以姊妹视之。且"娣"为媵婚制中之专名，其他之含义，多为引申或备用。以前之解释"娣"在亲属上之意义者，多离开媵婚而言，故不能得其真谛。[③]

"侄"之义，表现内侄女婚更为明显。"侄"在《尔雅》中为女子呼兄弟之子女之专称。《释亲·妻党》："女子谓晜弟之子为侄。"男子则呼姊妹之子为"出"。侄与姑为对称词，[④]《仪礼·丧服》："传

---

① 《左传》隐公元年："孟子卒，继室以声子。"杜注："诸侯始娶，则同姓之国以侄娣媵，元妃死则次妃摄治内事，犹不得称夫人，谓之继室。"此不过在理论上如此，事实上亦有不尽然者。

② 《公羊传》隐公七年："叔姬归于纪。"注："叔姬者，伯姬之媵也。"至是乃归者，待年父母之国也。

③ 如郑珍《巢经巢文集·娣似篇》即其一例也。

④ 对称词（reciprocity）之定义，参见拙著之《中国亲属制》（*The Chinese Kinship System*）170—171面。

曰：侄者，何也？谓吾姑者，吾谓之侄。"至于男子呼兄弟之子为侄则为媵婚停止后，字义上之转变（semantic change），其时约在魏晋之世，[1]侄为内侄女婿中之特别名词，观乎侄之原来解释，即可知之。《左传》僖十五年："侄其从姑"。虽侄可兼通男女，[2]则皆言从姑而嫁也。又《释名》所言，更为明显："姑谓兄弟之女为侄。姪，迭也。共行事夫，更迭进御也。"从现在之伦理观念视之，此乃何等荒谬之解释，刘熙若无所本，何敢出此谰言，淆乱尊卑，以致人伦失序。但自距刘熙不远之媵婚观之，此自为正当之诠释，与当时之伦常观念，固无所抵触也。

古代亲属名词中尚有一特征，可与内姪女婿相印证，即以前所论之"甥"是也。"甥"字之意义，除《尔雅》所言之姑之子，舅之子，妻之昆弟，及姊妹之夫外，《仪礼·丧服》言："甥者，何也？谓吾舅者，吾谓之甥。"[3]此乃言姊妹之子，而谓之曰甥。孟子又称女之夫曰甥。"舜尚见帝，帝馆甥于贰室……。"姊妹之子也，女之夫也，均与姑之子，舅之子，姊妹之夫，妻之昆弟，不仅行辈不同，且亦戚属各异，而一皆称之曰甥，其中必有大原因在也。

历来之注释家，均避开此问题，即有释之者，亦不得其要领。

---

① 《颜氏家训·风操篇》："兄弟之子已孤，与他人言对孤者前呼为兄子弟子，颇为不忍，北土人多呼为侄。"案《尔雅·丧服经》、《左传》侄名虽通男女，并是对姑之称，晋世以来，始呼叔侄。今呼为侄，于理为胜也。

② 此为两对称词中之特征。如"姑"对于所称亲属之性别，则指示明白，而对于称呼者（speaker）之性别，则无所知也。"侄"则对于所称亲属之性别，无所指示，而对于称呼者之性别，则曾明白指示也。故此两对称词之涵义中，每一词含有一种类别（category），而为其对面之词所无者。

③ 《尔雅·释亲》亦言："谓我舅者，吾谓之甥也。"但附于《婚姻》类之最末，可谓极无伦次，《释亲》之分类不合。其为后来误入之衍文，则可无疑。

如郝懿行之《尔雅·义疏》：

> 男子谓姊妹之子为出，又谓甥者，甥之言生，与出同义。故《释名》云："舅谓姊妹之子为甥，甥亦生也。"出配他男而生，故其制字，男旁作生。按上文云舅姑之子，妻之昆弟，姊妹之夫，俱谓之甥。彼谓敌体，此则同名而实异也。

"甥"一名词中各种意义之构成，并非由字义或字形可得解释，其后必有社会制度之背景。纵认"甥"与"出"之义同，而姊妹之子之"甥"，与"甥"之其他意义，尚须说明。郝氏不得已，乃以"同名而实异"含糊了之，而不能得其"同名"之所以然也。

案"出"为男子呼姊妹之子之原名，婿为女之夫之原名（《尔雅》女子子之夫为婿），"甥"者乃在内侄女婚制影响下所引申而来之新名。盖甥之本义为舅之子、姑之子、姊妹之夫及妻之兄弟。其姊妹之子，女之夫亦曰甥者，乃其后来之引申也。详而言之，在交表婚、姊妹交换婚及内侄女婚制之下，姊妹之子可与己之女为婚（交表婚），姊妹之夫亦可与己身之女为婚（内侄女婚），如是则姊妹之夫，姊妹之子，女之夫，在亲属关系上，实属相等。又如，舅之子与己身之姊妹为婚（交表婚），则亦可与己身之女为婚（内侄女婚）。故舅之子，姊妹之夫，女之夫，在亲属关系上亦属相等。综合言之，则舅之子，姑之子，姊妹之夫，妇之兄弟，姊妹之子，女之夫，在亲属上均为相等之关系。故用"甥"一名词以统之，亦无不可也。

由此可见姊妹同婚中之内姪女婚，表现于"姪"、"娣"及"甥"之名词上者，至为明显。不过以近代之伦理眼光视之，则似觉可骇，故宋人直有以媵婚之俗，实无其事，不过为汉儒所臆造者。但吾人自不能以现代之伦理观念绳古代之风俗，婚姻中之行辈限制，自魏晋以后始盛，魏晋以前，则无所拘也。[①]自人类社会学上视之，内姪女婚之俗，则更不足为怪，不只我国古时有之，现代之民族中，亦常见不鲜也。

收继婚

收继婚（levirate）之本义，为夫之兄弟婚。不过其在各民族中之变式，颇有不同。广泛之收继婚，兄死可以收嫂，弟亡可以娶弟妇；引申之，父死可以妻群母（生母除外），甚至祖亡亦可娶祖父之妻妾。狭义的而较普遍的收继婚，为夫亡时只可与夫之弟结婚，即俗所谓叔接嫂或转房是也，在人类学上则称曰Junior levirate。叔嫂婚之俗，在亚洲分布甚广，如印度、东北亚洲及中国境内之土著民族中，多有之。汉族之下级社会中亦有行之者，但不甚普遍耳。

---

① 不同行辈之亲属婚姻（inter-generation marriages），典籍所载，在魏晋以前，为例特多。如梁玉绳《瞥记》（卷二）所言："楚成王取文芈二女，（左僖廿二），晋文公纳嬴氏（僖廿四），皆因甥为妻者，可谓无别矣。"嗣后妻甥者，汉孝惠取张敖女，章帝取窦勋女，吴孙休取朱据女，俱楚颍晋重作之俑也。梁氏不明伦常观念进化之迹，故有是叹。此种不同行辈之婚姻，不只不为当时礼法所不禁，而言礼者，亦公开讨论。如《通典》（卷九五）所载族父是姨弟为服议，及娶同堂姊之女为妻，姊亡服议等是也。及至唐时，尚有行之者，如中宗娶其表姑为妻，《唐书》（卷七六）："中宗和思顺圣皇后赵……父环，尚高祖常乐公主，帝为英王，聘后为妃。"而在当时亦未有非议之者。

本义的收继婚，在分布上，多与姊妹同婚并行。即一民族中之有姊妹同婚者，多有收继婚；反之，有收继婚者，亦多有姊妹同婚之俗也。从现有之证据及亲属名词上观之，中国古时确有姊妹同婚之俗，再者，接近中国之各民族中，亦多有行叔嫂婚姻者，但在中国古时有无叔嫂婚姻之习，乃尚须研究之问题也。

格兰内即为主张中国古代有叔嫂婚者[1]，其所援之证据，《左传》庄公二十八年：

> 楚令尹子元欲蛊文夫人，为馆于其宫侧而振万焉。夫人闻之泣曰：先君以是舞也，习戎备也，令尹不寻诸仇雠，而于未亡人之侧，不亦异乎！

又定公十九年：

> 敝无存之父将室之，辞之以与其弟，曰：此役也，不死，反必娶于高国。

格兰内之援用此类证据，直等于无证据。子元之蛊息妫，不过为贪其色，并无娶嫂之义务，更非非娶其嫂后，始能得其兄之权力，而掌楚之国政也。至于敝无存之辞婚与弟，实因其心目中另有所属，欲娶于高氏国氏。其所辞之女，既非其妻，而其弟更非兄亡而收嫂，

---

[1]　参考 M.Granet, *La civilization chinois*, 424–425 页。

可谓与收继婚毫无关系。

格兰内又举丧服叔嫂无服为证，彼以为叔嫂无服，自然可以互为婚姻。不过服制一项，不能用作婚姻限制之标准，特别为小功以下之服，于婚姻无大阻碍，所谓"缌麻之服，不禁嫁娶"是也。

格兰内之必欲证中国中古有收继婚及姊妹同婚者，因彼以为收继婚及姊妹同婚为原始的群婚，即一群兄弟与一群姊妹结为婚姻之变相的遗留（survival）。如能证明收继婚及姊妹同婚之存在，则群婚制在中国古代之存在，可不证自明。格兰内之此种理论的推测，自高出国人之研究古代群婚及母系社会者一等，但其根据，亦援用摩尔根、泰洛耳（E.B.Tylor），及弗内色(Sir James Frazer)诸人之说，亦无所谓创见也。但以收继婚及姊妹同婚为群婚之遗，早为现在一般人类学者所否认。至于群婚一说，亦为有实地经验之人类学家所摒弃也。

施陈二氏所著之《中国亲属名词》一文中，[1]曾言"伯"一名词为收继婚之表现，因伯有"夫之兄"之义，而又有"丈夫"之义也。夫与夫之兄同统于一亲属名词之下，是夫之兄亦有作己身（女）丈夫之可能性（potential husband）也。考以"伯"作夫之义，则为《诗经·伯兮》：

> 伯兮朅兮，邦之桀兮；伯也执殳，为王前趋。自伯之东，首如飞蓬，岂无膏沐？谁适为容。

---

① J. K. Shryock and T. S. Chen, Chinese Relationship Terms, *American Anthropologist*, 34:4, 623–669, 其他如Ⅱ. p. Wilkinson之The Chinese Family Nomenclature, *New China Review (1921)*, 159–191, 则更卑卑不足道矣。

此处之"伯"，系指女子之夫而言。但"伯"之义，抑为称夫之亲属名词乎？夫之官爵乎？或呼夫之美称乎？均不甚明瞭。即使"伯"为称夫之亲属名词，亦不能用作为收继婚之证。因呼夫之兄为伯，最早亦不过起于五代之时也。

《尔雅》称夫之兄为兄公。公亦作伀，或作妐，读如锺。《释名》则作为兄章。章或作偉，或嫜。称夫之兄为伯，盖始于五代之时。陶岳《五代史补》卷五：

> （李）涛为人不拘礼法，与弟浣虽甚雍睦，然聚话之际，不典之言，往往间作。浣娶礼部尚书窦宁固之女，年甲稍高，成婚之夕，窦氏出参涛，辄望塵下拜。浣惊曰："大哥风狂耶？新妇参阿伯，岂有答礼仪？"涛应曰："我不风，只将是亲家母。"

自是之后，以"伯"称夫之兄之用渐广，及至现代，则蔚为通称。兄公、兄章之名，则鲜有知之者矣。由此可知以伯称夫，及以伯称夫之兄，不惟不同时，而且相距至少有一千余年之远，用之以作收继婚之证验，自属不当。

收继婚在礼法上之禁止，为时甚早，亦且甚严厉。古代与汉族接触之民族有此俗者，亦早知之。史家每引为异俗，而不齿其于人类。如《史记·匈奴列传》所记之："父死妻其后母，兄弟死皆取其妻妻之。"是也。至于法律之禁，唐以前不可知，现在所存最早之完全法典《唐律疏议》户婚条下：

诸尝为袒免亲而嫁娶者，各杖一百。缌麻及舅甥妻，徒一年。小功以上以奸论。妾各减二等，并离之。

在此律令之下，各种之收继婚，自属不可能，而其罚亦不可谓不重，所谓奸者，即 incest 之谓也。至于明律，则更为明白严厉，《明律集解》户婚："若收祖父妾及伯叔母者，各斩。兄亡收嫂，弟亡收弟妇者，各绞。"清律亦全与此相同。间尝推之，明律之所以特别标明者，大概系由于元人收继婚传入中国后之一种反响，亦未可知。

春秋时代及春秋以后，史籍所载之上蒸下报之事，为例甚多，然皆不能视为收继婚之遗，乃为例外之事也。因其大都皆出于贪慕女子之色，而非出于娶之之义务也。正当之收继婚俗，如兄没之后，不管嫂之有色与否，或己身已娶与否，均须收嫂为妻，不然者，则无以对亡兄，对寡嫂，对亲戚，而将为社会所不齿。再者，或视女子为财产，防其外溢，则惟有收继之一途。细考典籍中所载，均无此类观念之遗留或表现。若为一时财色所驱使，则随时随地均可发生，不必为收继婚俗之表现也。

结论

由以上所论之各点观之，中国古代婚俗之表现在亲属名词上者，以交表婚姻为最肯定，姊妹同婚及内侄女婚次之，至于收继婚则全无征验。[①]媵婚（即姊妹同婚及其引伸之内侄女婚）随封建制度以俱去，秦汉以后则无闻。经典中对于此婚俗之记载虽多，但以其制度之奇特，后之学者对之，疑信参半，鲜有能明瞭其真实意义者。今得亲属名词上之征验，其在中国古代婚制中之重要意义，则可以概见矣。

交表婚姻，自秦汉而后，行之者颇多，普通称为"中表婚"。但为一种"许可式"的，而非"指定式"的婚俗，故于现代之亲属名词中，则无所表现。交表婚制之失掉其"强制性"，大概在春秋以前，或在殷周之际。因至秦汉之时，《尔雅》中所释"舅"、"姑"、"甥"之义，已与当时亲属关系之实际不合。而需要新兴名词以代之。如妐（夫之父）见《吕氏春秋》，[②]尊章（夫之父）见《汉书》及《释名》，[③]中表、[④]内兄弟、[⑤]外兄弟、[⑥]妇公[⑦]等名词均始于汉。至魏晋以后新起之名词代替"舅"、"姑"、"甥"之各种意义者更繁，而交表婚姻，亦已开始为礼法所禁止矣。

（原载《齐鲁学报》第 1 期，1941 年）

---

① 中国现代下层社会中所行之少数嫂婚，大概系受外族之影响。可参见：*China Review*. 10（1881–2），71, *The levirate in China*; P. G. von Mollondorff, *The Family Law of The Chinese*, 1896；黄华节：《叔接嫂》，《东方杂志》31：7（1934）；及李鲁人：《元代蒙古收继婚俗传人内地之影响》，《大公报》史地周刊，廿五年四月十日，第八期。

② 《吕氏春秋》卷一四慎人篇：姑妐知之曰：为我妇而有外心。

③ 《汉书》卷五三，广川王去传："背尊章嫖以忽。"师古曰："尊章，犹言舅姑也。"今关中俗妇呼舅为锺。锺者，尊声之转也。《释名・释亲属》：俗或谓舅曰章，又曰妐。

④ 《后汉书・郑太传》："公业惧，乃诡词更对曰……又名公将帅，皆中表腹心。"

⑤ 《仪礼・丧服》："舅之子。"郑注："内兄弟也。"

⑥ 《仪礼・丧服》："姑之子。"郑注："外兄弟也。"

⑦ 《后汉书・第五伦传》："帝戏谓伦曰：'闻乡为吏篣妇公，不过从兄饭，宁有之耶？'伦对曰：'臣三娶妻皆无父。'"

评张仲实译本恩格斯
《家族、私有财产及国家的起源》

（三联书店1950年2月第一版）

恩格斯这一经典的名著，在以前国内出版界中已经有过两种译本，张仲实先生的这一译本，是第三种了。张先生的这一译本，较之以前的两种，诚然是进步得多了，不过其中还有好多地方，尚可商讨。因为诚如张先生所说："古典的理论著作，大抵文字艰深，很难翻译，拙译本中不完善之处一定还是有的，读者如有发现，还希给以善意的指教！"张先生这种虚心的态度，是可令人佩服的，所以我根据张先生这种可敬的态度，把译文中的若干地方，举出来与张先生略一商榷。

张先生的这一译本，据他的译者序言中说："是根据莫斯科马恩列学院院长亚多拉茨基所重新校阅及所编辑注释的俄文标准译本译来的。"不过恩格斯的此书，原本为德文，而亚多拉茨基的俄文译本，是根据第四版德文本，现在在成都无从得到德文原本，所以我只好用Alick West与Dona Torr合译的英文本校阅，因为他们的译本是根据1934年莫斯科第四版德文本译来的。好在恩格斯此书，主要的是根据莫尔根的《古代社会》，此为英文本，这是可以校阅的。

恩格斯此书最重要的部分，可以说是第二章，即论家族的一章。以篇幅论，约占全书三分之一而强（如全书译文连序共200面，此一章则占77面），此一章也可以说是全书理论的关键，也是最难翻译的一章。因为它大半所根据的，是人类的亲属制度；而亲属制度，是民族学中最专门、最枯燥、最准确及最难了解的一部分。人类学家往往戏呼亲属制度为"亲属代数"，因为其应用，有似代数之于数学，其繁难于此可知！我们须知道，亲属制度与社会制度的关系，及利用亲属制度来推演社会制度的发展是莫尔根的千古独发之秘，替社会发展的研究上，打开了一条新道路。因为这一原因及本刊的篇幅的限制，本文的商讨，将以这一章为主要。

张先生把类分式的亲属制（Classificatory system）翻译成"阶级制度"，这是与莫尔根、恩格斯的原意不合的。例如43面："氏族制度，在大多数场合下，似乎是从'普那路亚'家族中发生的。是的，澳大利亚人的阶级制度（澳大利亚人是有氏族的）也可以成为氏族的出发点……"又如45面："它本身是比澳大利亚阶级更高的一个发展阶段。"这两处恩格斯都是指澳大利亚人的类分式的亲属制所代表的婚姻阶级（Marriage classes），而不指仅仅的阶级，因为澳大利亚人是没有像我们社会中的阶级的。

类分式的亲属制（Classificatory system）是亲属制度研究上最专门的名词，是莫尔根创的，凡是原文用此者，绝没有译作阶级制度的可能的。为要说明这一点，我们须要将莫尔根的家庭发展阶段稍为说明一下。莫尔根把家族的发展分成五个阶段：

家庭形态　　　　　　　　　　　亲属制度

(一)血缘家庭　　　——　　　　马来亚式　　⎫
　　　　　　　　　　　　　　　　　　　　　　⎬ 类分式（Classificatory）
(二)群婚家族（即普那路亚家族）——图南式　⎭

(三)对偶家族

(四)父权家族

（五）单偶家族（即一夫一妻家族）——亚利安式——叙述式（Descriptive）

关于这五种家庭形态，照莫尔根的意思，只有第一、第二及第五种是基本形态，是革命性的变革。因为这三种中的每一种，都各自创造出了一种独特的亲属制度。如血缘家庭则有其马来亚式亲属制（Malayan system），群婚家族则有图南式亲属制（Turanian system），单偶家族则有其亚利安式亲属制（Arayn system），至于第三（对偶家族）与第四（父权家庭）两种家庭，即不曾创出新的亲族制度，也不曾对于当时存在的亲属制度予以本质的改变，故莫尔根与恩格斯称之为中间形态或过渡形态。再者马来亚式及图南式两种，又称之为类分式，因为它们的特征，是将旁系亲属混合在直系亲属以内，分成若干类别而统称之。亚利安式亲属制，又称为叙述式，因为它的特征，是把旁系亲属与直系亲属描述得极为清晰，而不类称之。我们若明乎此，所以凡有原文用 Classificatory 的，要当亲属制度上的专门名词翻译，不可译作"阶级制度"。

现在我们把亲属制度的总原则稍为说明以后，我们来看张先生对于亲属称谓的翻译了。在家族这一章的第一面（全书29面）张先生译道："易洛魁人的男子，不仅把自己亲生的小孩称为子女，而且把他的兄弟的小孩也称为子女，而小孩把他们称为父。他把自己的姊妹的小孩，称为自己的侄子和侄女，他们称他为叔父。适为相反，易洛魁人的女子，把自己姊妹以及她自己亲生的小孩称为子及女，他们称她为母。她们把自己兄弟的小孩称为侄子和侄女，她自己被称为他们的叔母。同样，兄弟的小孩们，互称为兄弟姊妹，姊妹的小孩们，也是如此。反之，一个妇女的和她的兄弟的小孩互称为从兄弟及从兄妹。"这是三重翻译。恩格斯把易洛魁人的亲属称谓译成印欧语系称谓（所谓亚利安式），张先生又从印欧语的亲属称谓译成汉语的亲属称谓，所以在我们中国人看来，就格格不入了。因为我们中国亲属称谓要比西人的称谓来得密致些，辨别性要强些。例如 Uncle 一词，可以称之伯、叔父、舅父、姨父及姑夫。Aunt 一词，可以称之伯叔母、姨母及姑母。Nephew 一词，可称侄子、外甥及内侄子。Niece 一词，可称侄女、外甥女及内侄女。Cousin 一词则不分性别，可称堂兄弟及表（姑舅表）兄弟姊妹等等。现在我们再看易洛魁人的亲属称谓如何？例如一易洛魁人，己身（男）称姊妹之子为 ha-ya-wan-da，称姊妹之女为ka–ya–wan–da。已身（女）称兄弟之子为ha–sob–neh，兄弟之女为ka–sob–neh。分别亟为明晰。恩格斯以nephew及niece两词统之，这在恩格斯是可通的，因为在印欧语系中并不加以区别故也。若照欧语不加区别译成汉语，则要发生混淆，因为汉语亲属称谓又严格加以区别故也。又如易洛魁人兄弟之子女称己身（女）为ah–ga–buc，恩格斯译为aunt，是可通的。如换张先生的汉译为叔母，那就不能通了。因为易洛魁人的称谓中称叔母（父之弟之妻）为uc–nog–ese，与父之姊妹的称呼，截然不同，如何能混为一谈？再就亲属的性质言，二者亦截然不同。姑母为血亲，而叔母为姻亲，后者与己身并无血缘关系。所以我把这一段的亲属称谓通篇改译如后：

> 易洛魁人的男子，不仅把自己亲生的小孩称为子女，而且把他的兄弟的小孩也称为子女，而小孩们把他称为父。他们把自己的姊妹的小孩称为外甥子和外甥女，他们称他为舅父。适为相反，易洛魁人的女子，把自己姊妹以及她自己亲生的小孩称为子女，他们称她为母。她把自己兄弟的小孩称为内侄子和内侄女，她自己被称为他们的姑母。同样，兄弟的小孩们互称为兄弟姊妹，姊妹的小孩们，也是如此。反之，一个妇女的小孩和她的兄弟的小孩，互称为表兄弟及表姊妹。

这样，在中国的亲属称谓上，才可以贯通。不过此中还有几个问题，为明白起见，不能不在此稍为说明一下。张先生译

"舅""甥"与"姑""侄"为"叔""侄"，亦是犯了三重转译的毛病，不明了易洛魁人及中国亲属制的特征。舅与甥为"对称词"，"谓吾舅者，吾谓之甥"。姑与侄为"对称词"，"谓吾姑者，吾谓侄"。这是表现易洛魁人的舅权制（avunclate）及甥权制（nepotic succession）。因为在易洛魁人中，自己（男子）的子女，不能承袭自己的财产与爵位，只有姊妹的子女，即外甥，才能承袭自己的财产与爵位，这是母系氏族的特征，自巴可芬以来就已经知道了的。再者张先生把兄弟的子女与姊妹的子女的互称译为从兄弟从姊妹，这也是不合的。因为在易洛魁人从兄弟即兄弟，从姊妹即姊妹，因为在他们的类分式的亲属制中，是无"堂从"之分的，故当译为"表"。"堂从"同氏同族而不能通婚，"表"则不同氏族而可以通婚。

　　总之，张先生的翻译，竟把亲属称谓弄成了矛盾的一团，这大概是张先生对于亲属制度的研究，未有搞透彻的缘故。不过我们须知道，亲属制是莫尔根及恩格斯推论最早家族发展的最主要的论证，若是把它弄混淆了，那就无法推论了。再者不只这一段是如此，后面的若干亲属称谓，都要依据原称谓对照汉语称谓加以移译，不能用欧语称谓随便加以移译了。

　　中国人是一个最注意亲属制度的民族，这是因封建时代的家族，是建立在亲属制度之上的。历来关于这一类的著作也很多，也有一套专门名词。《尔雅》中的释亲，可算是最早的代表，《礼记》中有亲属记（佚篇），《仪礼》中的丧服传，差不多完全是讲亲属的。以后历代关于小学、礼及类书中，几乎都有言亲属专篇。中国人既然是如此注意亲属关系，所以我想我们若是翻译这类性质的东西时，也不妨顾到已有的专门名词，至少在翻译时，名词要统一，方不致混淆。例如"亲属制度"张先生往往译为"血族制度"，这是可以商榷的。因为亲属里面实包括血亲（consanguineal relatives）与姻亲（affinal relatives 即亲属关系由婚姻关系而建立者）两大类别。这在《尔雅》中就已经划分，而莫尔根区分得更为清楚。故"血族制度"等等名词，并不是"亲属制度"的好代名词，也不能概括全体。

其他专门名词的翻译，亦多可议之处。例如34面第12行，张先生把polygamy译成"一夫多妻制"，这是一般通俗的译法，而没有顾到这一词的专门涵义。按polygamy一词，可包括两种，一为一夫多妻（polygamy），一为一妻多夫（polyandry）；而群婚者，则为男子多妻而同时女子多夫而已。故polygamy一词，亦可概括多妻、多夫与群婚，当译作"多偶制"。而厄斯皮那斯在此处实泛指群婚，张先生译成"一夫多妻制"把恩格斯所引的厄斯皮那斯这一段，弄得几乎不可理解了。所以这一名词的翻译，当看其上下文的涵义如何，不能只照一般的以"一夫多妻"概译之。而恩格斯在全书中应用它，也是很为明白的。

又如张先生把moiety译作"阶级"，把phratry译作"大氏族"，这似乎未曾明了民族学上的术语。Moiety的意义为"一半"，故当译为"半族"，有译者译为"分族"，系由"双分制（dual organization）"而来，因半族又称为双分制也。如澳大利亚人的部落中，有的分成四个婚姻阶级，有的分成八个婚姻阶级，此四婚姻阶级或八婚姻阶级，又各分成两个外婚的团体，这就是"分族"了。又如易洛魁人中有六个部落，除一个部落外，其余五个部落，都各分成两个分族，如山利加部落中有八个氏族，而分成两个分族，每分族包含四个氏族。再如一个部落中的各氏族，分成两个以上的集团时，则称为"胞族（phratty）"。如在古代希腊的亚蒂加，共有4个部落，每个部落各有90个氏族，此各90个氏族又分成3个胞族，每胞族各有30个氏族。故在应用上，分族可以称为胞族，而胞族绝不能称为分族。这在恩格斯用来，是极为有规律的。

以上所举的，不过是几个例子而已，其他类似的情形尚多。又往往同一名词，恩格斯在全书中，都用作一个意义，而译文中则使用不同的名词，这也徒增混淆，使读者不易捉摸。总之，恩格斯这本不朽的名著，诚如张先生所说，是不容易翻译的。因为恩格斯极为博洽，取材极广，故翻译这一名著，不仅要以能通晓它的文字为已足，还必须对于它有关的科学有相当的准备，才能译好。

现在我们看看张先生的译文了，可惜我得不到德文原本，加以校对，好在恩格斯书中引有英、法、德等国的图籍，这有时可以找到原文，是可以对核的。例如49面引莫尔根说：

```
The influence of the new practice, which brought
unelated persons into marriage relations, tended to
create a mere vigorous stock physically and mentally…
When two advancing tribes, with strong mental and physical
```

characters, are brought together and blended into one people by the accidents of barbarous(o？)life, the new skull and brain woulds widen and lengthen to the sum of the capabilities of both.

张译：未构成一个血缘关系的各氏族成员间之婚姻，产生了在肉体上及精神上更强健的人种；两种进步的部落混合以后，下一代的头盖与脑髓，便自然而然地扩大起来，直到他们联合了两个部落的能力为止。

改译：这种新风俗的影响，使无（血缘）关系的个人进入婚姻关系，倾向于创造一心身更健壮的血统……当两个具有强健心灵及体质特征的进展的部落，由于野蛮生活的偶然性，使其接近而混合成为一个民族时，他们新（一代）的头骨及脑髓，必将加宽加长，直达到两族的可能的综合为止。

张先生的这一段翻译，并没有十分大错，不过离原文太远一些罢了。再者，译者为要使译文更明确起见，凡原文中为行文之便所省略的，在译文中必需所加入者，必须放在括号以内，使读者明了其原为原文所略。

又如第60面引莫尔根：

The organization of a number of persons, bond and free, into a family under paternal power, for the purpose

of holding lands, and for the care of blocks and herds…(In
the semitic form)the chiefs, at least, lived in polygamy…
Those held to servitude, and those employed as slaves, lived
in the marriage relation.

张译：若干数目的自由人及非自由人组织起来而成为一个父权的家长权力的家庭。在塞姆人中，这个一家之长是过着一夫多妻的生活，非自由人也有妻和子，而整个组织的目的是在于在一定地域范围以内照管畜群。

改译：一群非自由的与自由的若干个人，在父权之下，组织成一个家族，其目的为占有土地及照管羊群与牛群……（在塞姆人的形态中）至少酋长是多妻……那些被缚束为奴役的及那些被雇为仆役的，在这婚姻关系之下，共同生活（或居住）。

恩格斯虽然把这一段中的原文略去了若干部分，但在文义上还是很清楚的。张先生大概是未把上下文看清楚，Lived in the marriage relation，并不是指"非自由人也有妻和子"，而是指父权家长的婚姻关系。当然奴役也可以有妻子，但不是指他们而言，这是很明白的。占有土地及照管畜群，是两件事，并不是"在一定地域范围以内照管畜群"。这也很清楚。

又如59面引马克思的评语：

Man's innate casuistry！ To change things by changing

their names! And to find loopholes for violating tradition whilst maintaining tradition, when direst interest supplied sufficient impulse.

张译：人类的天赋的决疑法是更改名称，以改变事物，并找出一个间隙，以便在传统的范围以内打破传统，其时直接的利益便对于这作了充分的鼓舞。

改译：人类生来的诡辩！用改变它们的名称来变更事物！当直接利益供给了足够的冲动时，就是维持传统中去找空隙来破坏传统。

因为马克思在语句上稍为前后倒置，就把张先生弄迷糊了。再者这是写按语常有的句法，短小精悍，并不是什么难解的语句。

以上所举的，已可见张先生译文的一般，其他的很多地方，译文的意义往往不能通贯，可惜没有德文原文对照，但在英文译本中，却是很清楚的。例如74面张先生译道：

随着个体婚姻而出现了两种不变的，为以前所不知道的特殊的社会典型：妻的常住的情人与奸妇之夫。男子虽获得了对妇女的胜利，但是荣冠还是由败者泰然承受了。

此一段最后的一句，显然与前面所说的不相照应，照英文译文应该是：

男子虽获得了对女子的胜利，但失败者却很慷慨的献以绿头巾的荣冠。

这样，才与前面所说的两种社会典型：（1）常伴着妻的情人，（2）王八丈夫，相照应。并不是"荣冠还是由败者（女子）泰然承受了"。

像这样的例子，译文中尚有不少，不过限于副刊的篇幅，不能尽行列举。但在好多地方，张先生显系弄错了。如第75面恩格斯引傅立叶说：

如在法文上，两个否定成为一个肯定一样，在婚姻理论上，两种卖淫则构成一种美德了。

傅立叶固系法人，然何止法文是如此！所有的文法，又何尝不是如此？故此处应为"如在文法上两个否定成为一个肯定一样……"（英译本即是如此）张先生特在法字旁边打了一直杠，正误表上亦未更正，想不是手写之误了。

又如第36 ~ 37面"印度支那加勒皮人（Cariheans）……"按：加勒皮人并不在印度支那，而是在南美洲东北靠加勒比海（Carihean sea）。第45面"在南澳大利亚甘比亚（Gambier）山区澳洲黑人（Papuans）中……"这一"Papuans"从何而来？按：巴卜安人是新几内亚（New Guinea）的黑人，绝不能到澳洲去。不知俄文译本中有此注吗？这些都是小误，需要检查原本而加以改正的。

拉杂的写了许多了，不过对整个的译本，尚需要讲几句话。自整个的译文看来，时常感觉张先生的翻译过于自由了。在许多地方，往往随意增省，又往往将句法作不必要的颠倒，原文的意义虽然是勉强表达出了，但是距离原文则太远。由前面所举的几个例子，就可以看出一些。记得阿尔多利治《论〈马哥孛罗游记〉翻译》的一段话说得很好，大意谓"照两种文字不同的距离所能允许者，愈直译愈佳。照这种方法，原著者的才力可以让他表现出来，他的坚定可见的努力来表白他的意思，也不至于被隐蔽了"。这种方法，也可以用来翻译恩格斯的这本名著，因为这一部天才横溢，意义深远，论证精确的理论杰作，其结论往往远出乎莫尔根之上，至于措辞之坚定，又特其余事。例如恩格斯精确地论证了血缘家族以后而加以结论说："夏威夷的亲属制迫使我们不能不承认这种家族必定是存在过的。"又在"必定"上特加上着重号，以表示其坚定的意思，而张先生译为"不过，夏威夷的亲族制度，使我们不能不承认这种家族大概是存在过的"。"必定"与"大概"在字的数目上虽是相等的，但变"肯定"为"或然"，远失去了恩格斯的论证的力量了，而在"大概"旁虽加上着重号，那末，恩格斯亦不能自信他的结论是正确了！又有什么意义呢？我深知道，批评别人是很容易的，自己作来却是很困难。所以我对张先生的译本并不是"吹毛求疵"的苛求，而实是因为恩格斯这一千古不朽的杰作，在国内出版界中，应该有一本比较可靠的译本，以供一般人的研读。所以我愿意据我所知道的，写出一点意见，以供张先生的参考，想张先生也当为首肯。不过我见到的，也不一定是正确的，还希望大家加以指正。

（原载成都《工商导报》1951 年 1 月 21 日《学林》副刊第二期）

中国文化发展的南向与北向说的新论

　　近来研究中国文化问题的，有时注意到中国文化发展中方向，即向南与向北发展的问题。此一问题在中国文化的孳育及构成上，自然有相当的重要性，因为在一种文化发展的方向中，实包括环境的变迁、民族的接触以及文化的交流等等问题，因而影响整个文化的内容与结构。现在这个问题的研究，可以说刚在萌芽之中，文献并不甚多，其中比较有价值的要以日人桑原骘藏的《由历史上观察的中国南北文化》[①]（杨筠如译，《国立武汉大学文哲季刊》一卷三号），张振之的《中国文化之南向开展》（《新亚细亚杂志》一卷三期），梁园东的《现代中国的北方与南方》（《新生命》三卷十二期），及陈序经的《南北文化的真谛》（见陈氏所着《中国文化的出路》第七章）。

　　以上各论文的大意，均以为中国文化在历史上的发展，系由北

---

① 原文正文述及之专著、论文或期刊，均未加书名号。整理者整理时均添加了书名号。下同，不另注。

而南，特别自永嘉乱后，其南趋的动向，较前尤为加速。但自海通以后，中国之文化发展的动向，则完全掉转来变为由南而北。他们在各方面举出若干事实，以为佐证，不过我们在此处不必一一加以阐述，因本文的目的，并不在阐明或推翻此种学说，而本文所要研求的，是中国文化发展中之所以动向及其转变的原因，所以注重在原理阐述，而不在事实搜集。

中国文化的发展先由北而南，现在则为南而北的原因，在上面所举的论文中，亦稍有论及者，如梁园东氏以为中国文化的发展在历史上有北而南的原因，是属于经济的，这当然我们不能完全否认，否过未（原文如此）离地理环境论的窠臼，实不足以解释中国文化之动向也。陈序经氏则以为北方文化，是中国固有的文化，而南方文化则是西洋的文化，中国固有文化的发展，系由北而南，而西洋文化的传来，则系由南而北。陈氏似乎明白一点其中的道理，而实际上实不能捉摸其所谓动向的"真谛"何在也。

研究文化发展的动向，并不是一种新的探讨，特别在地理环境论中此说为最早，文化向冷的方向移动，在欧洲即早有此说，例如以欧洲文化的发展史观之，则皆发源于温暖的南方，逐渐向寒冷的北方移动。如埃及苏墨为西方文明进步之最早者，埃及苏墨衰，巴比仑、克里特、腓力基、亚叙利亚等继之而起；巴比仑等之文化衰，则有西腊、罗马兴起；西腊、罗马之文化衰，现代之北欧文明乃继之而兴。故从整个文化发展史上观之，文化的动向，是朝北冷的方向走的，在欧西文化的进展整个历史中自然亦不乏例外，而向南游移，但均为暂时的，与当文化衰落之际，倘若文化继续向前进步，则仍然转而向北移动，此时我们若试问欧西文化的发展，为什么总是向北方推进？根据此说的解答，其原因完全为气候（即环境）。因为文化进步，对于环境的管制愈趋严密，以前所谓寒冷地带，不适于文化的发展者，现在因为文化的进步变为最宜于文化发展的地带。所以说文化愈为进步，则愈向寒冷的地带进展。

此说在骤然间视之，颇觉动听，不过文化的发展，决不是如此简单，完全受环境的支配的。环境当然是文化发展最重要因子之一，但不是惟一的因子。文化的动向与进展，其中尚有其他的成分，是不受环境决定的。此处自不是详细批评此说的地方，不过借以指出研究文化问题上一种趋向而已。

在世界文化的进展上，欧西的文化，是向寒冷的北方发展；东方的中国文化，是向温暖南方发展。这种相反的动向，自不是环境一项可以说明的了，我们要解释这个问题，需要将旧大陆（包括亚非欧）整个文化的传播问题加以检讨，方可明了。因为这个问题，根本是一个文化的传播问题与民族之迁徙问题，而地理环境不过其背景之一而已。

我们知道一种文化的生长与增加繁富，十九是依靠传播。一种文化中的各种特征（Traits），其为本文化中所发明者，十常不得一二。例如以我们中国文化而言，我们若将我们之文化中的成分详细加以分析而溯其来源，恐怕很少是我们中国人自己发明的。我们可将现代从欧输入的各种机械文化撇开不说，只以所谓中国固有的文化而言，即可以明了了。以中国的食物（一种文化的经济基础）而言，例如米，是我们南方重要的食品，而米是我们中国的发现吗？不是的，米的最早的种植，大概是在印度或巴比伦，在新石器时代始传至中国（以现在考古学上所知，在新石器时代末期在河南仰韶已知种稻）。玉蜀黍与蕃薯，是美洲印第安人的农作物，至明代始入中国，这是有记载可稽的，然而这不是中国若干地方的主要食物吗？再进一步，我们若将中国其他主要农作品（所谓五谷）一一追溯其来源，其中恐怕没有一种是原在中国地方种植的，或最早为中国人种植的。然而我们岂不是常常自傲的说，我们是以农立国吗？我们文化的基本特征是农业吗？简而言之，我们若将我们文化中的成分，自外面传入者提出，自己发明者留下，我想我们将要回返到原始的旧石器时代了，这并不是过言，而是事实。所以说一种文化倘不受外界传播的影响，不止其内容无从增加丰富，亦无从生长，根本就不肯进步。现在地球上各边远地带文化落后民族，并非他们创造文化的能力不如其他高级文化的民族，实是因为他们处于边远地带，外面的发明传播不到他们当中罢了。

　　中国文化南进的问题，亦是一个文化传播的问题。中国文化为什么要先南进而后变为北进？此问题的解答及总括言之，不过是世界文化传播的路线转变而已。我们若问，文化传播的路线为什么要转变？讲起来这也很简单，这是文化自身发展的结果。自新石器时代以来，旧大陆的文化的重心，是埃及、两河间，印度河及黄河流域。这四处的文化，在传播上，是互相影响，又均建筑在一共同的原始文化基础之上。再者，这四处文化在其传播上即互相影响上，均以中亚为其交通的孔道。例如中国自新石器以来以至海道未开以前，泰平之文化上的传播，均来自从中亚而来的西方；而西方的两河间及埃及则反是。民族上的迁徙，亦复如是。此在历史上考古学上，可以找出充分的证据，此处因为限于篇幅，不能详细的讨论了。

然而，文化传播，并不是单方面的，随便那一种文化，都是一方面接受外来的文化特征，又一方面将已有的文化特征，传播出去，中国文化当然亦是如此。例如中国文化中的特征，在早如丝，在后如纸张、印刷、火药、指南针等，均系由中亚而传往西方。

现在我们既说明文化的生长，主要是靠传播，而旧世界的文化重心间的主要传播方向及路线，亦已稍为说明，现在我们可以讨论文化重心之移动方向了。

历史常常告诉我们，世界上的文化重心，时时在那里移动，往往一种文化在某一地发展至相当时间之后，又移往他处。这种现象，不只旧世界是如此，新世界的高级文化，亦复如是，如玛雅（Maya）及亚兹特克（Aztec）等文化是也。文化重心之移动的动向，（一）靠文化传播的方向，（二）民族移动的方向，（三）地理的背景。明乎此三者，文化发展的动向，可得其大半了。现在我们可先讨论中国文化为什么要向东南发展？

前已言过，中国文化在传播上所得各种文化的新特征，系由中亚这一条交通大道，换言之，即由西至东。此并非说从东南一方面中国文化毫未得到新的文化特征，实际上中国文化包含东南文化的成分，亦复不少，此不过讲中国文化所受之主要的影响，是从西北而已。文化上自西至东的这种传播方向，不只在物资方面是如此，在文化的其他各方面，亦莫不是如此。以宗教而言，如佛教、早期耶教、回教等，均自西北陆路以入中国。

自民族之迁徙上言之，其主要方向，亦为自西北而向东南，在历史前如罗底克人（Nordic）及亚尔班人（Alpine）中各混合种之东向迁徙，波南尼西亚人之南入太平洋，其路线皆必需经过东亚者。在历史期间，举其最著者而言，如秦汉之匈奴，两晋六朝之五胡，唐之突厥，宋之辽金元，其压力的方向，均系自西或北，以向东或南。当汉族的抵抗力量强盛时，当然他们不能越雷池一步，但是当汉族衰弱的时候那就不能不被迫南迁，东晋与南宋就是当中最好的例子。当然，民族的迁徙，其中亦当然包括文化的移动了。

文化与民族的发展动向，前已言之，地理的环境，亦为当中的因子之一。我们若把亚洲的地形一看，横断东亚中部的，为一广大的沙漠。我从历史上面看，知道沙漠是文化与民族移动上的大障碍。甚至于现代高度机械化的文化中，通过广大的沙漠，有时亦非易事，其在以前为人类交通上阻碍力之大，是可想而知的。沙漠当中，除了少数沃原（Oasis），或缘边的草原地带可以存留少数的游牧民族而外，是不能发生高级文化的。所以在传播上自西而东的中国的文化，北方有沙漠的大阻碍，除了向东向南发展以外，实别无其他的途径。实际上，中国文化发展途径，亦只有这两种方向。中国比较早期的文化发展是在山西、陕西、河南一带，其后逐渐向东发展，其萌（？）

哨（？）①实达于高丽、日本，此在近代的考古上已得充实的证明。然而中国文化根本为大陆文化，不惯利用海洋交通的机会，故其对洋海，不只不能视为一种便利，反而为一种阻碍，那末它最易发展的方向，为折而向南。再者中国文化为一种高级农业文化，而南方热湿肥沃，兼有长江及珠江流域的冲积平原，其土壤之肥沃，气候之宜于农业，实驾乎黄河流域而上之，故中国文化之向南发展，自为自然之趋势了。加以世界文化传播的动向，民族流动的压力，欲求中国文化之北移，实不可得也。

中国文化的南向发展，既然是如此，那末，自明清以后为什么掉转头来由南而北呢？这个问题的解答，骤然视之，颇为矛盾，其实亦颇简单，即世界文化传播的路径及方向转变了是也。自从十五世纪之末，科仑布发现新大陆而后，探险之风大行，其后造船航海等术进步，海洋交通益行发达。从前西方文化由中亚而传至中国西北者，现在则由海道而先至东南，俟东南接受以后，再传播到西北。从前中国与西方的交通孔道中亚细亚，自明清而后，几完全蔽塞，甚而有人不知有此一回事者，从前的东南是中国文化的尾巴，现在则西北变成中国文化的尾巴了。再者中国自秦汉而后，文化的重心渐向东南移动，其结果，至明清之时，东南的文化，实高于西北的文化。文化的传播，虽为交互的，低级文化自高级文化接受文化的特征，而高级文化，亦自低级文化吸收其所无。但文化之传播，亦犹水然，每从高而就下，此不过譬而言之，即低者从高者接受较多是也。所以从世界文

---

① 此二字原文模糊不清。

化传播路线上的转变上而看，及从中国文化本身发展上而看，虽然地理的环境无殊于前，而文化发展的动向，实不能不掉转过头来了。

　　　　　　　　　　［原载《学思》第三卷第六期（1943 年）］

论东西文化

人类文化是否可分"东""西"？自文化的本身看来，实在是很有问题。当然，我们为研究的方便起见，不妨把人类的文化分为若干类型，以便我们容易了解整个人类文化的生长现象。此种方法，自是无可非议。不过现在一般研究中国文化的，竟把文化分作"东方"与"西方"，当作一种目的，而不是一种手段，实有乖于文化学的本旨，无怪乎我们谈了许多年的东方文化，愈谈愈不明白。

什么是文化

什么是文化？现在实有一说的必要。因为此名词的滥用，可说已经远到极点。人人都在谈文化，而各人有各人的文化定义，所以彼此永远谈不拢来。别的不用说了，即以本刊创号姜蕴刚先生的《东方文化论》①而言，首先即将文化与文明分开，文化是属于精神的范围，文明是属于物质的范围。此在姜先生固然是属于创见，但就姜先生所下的定义而言，他所谈的还是东方的精神文化，而不是整体的东方文化。

"文化"一词所指的是什么？在人类学上是有固定的范围的，用不着每一次来自下一界说。不过现在为了明瞭起见，不妨把它提出来。我们也用不着详征博引，就着最早泰洛尔对文化所下的界说为何？泰洛尔说："文化是一个复杂总和，包括知识、信仰、艺术、道德、法律、习俗，以及人类以社会之一员的资格，所获得的其他一切能为与习惯"。由此，可以见文化实包括人类社会生活的全体（生理的除外），并无所谓精神的与物质的区分。研究时，有时虽可将各部门分开来说，但全是为了研究的方便，文化的本身是不允许分割的，因为那一种文化一分割，那一种文化就不存在了。

后来的人类学家在文化界说上虽各有用的字句上的不同，但对于文化的根本观念，与泰洛尔则是完全一致的。抽象的说来，文化即是人类的"社会遗传"。因为人类在它的进展中，同时有两种遗传在进行，一是生物的遗传，凡我们体质上的特征以及本能上的行为均属之，其传递系由遗传素（germ pasm）上面传递，再一种即是社会的遗传，是遗传素以外的一种遗传，包括所有一切学习的行为，及经过社会约制的本能行为。因其传递完全系由于社会的中介而传递，故称之曰社会遗传，亦即是文化。

---

① 原文无书名号，书名号系整理者所加。

再者，文化与文明有分别吗？在人类学及社会学上是彼此互用，而不加区别的。不过有些人用"文明"代表一些进步的文化，如中国文明、印度文明、西洋文明；用"文化"以代表比较原始的文化，如印第安文化、亚斯基摩文化。是因为文化与文明有此类"价值论"的用法，故在人类学及社会学中只用"文化"而少用"文明"一名词。至于把"文化"与"文明"加以另外的区别，是玄学上的把戏，与研究人类文化的人类学及社会学是不相干涉的。

精神文化与物质文化

现在之研究东西文化的，大半多以为东方文化重精神，西方文化重物质，前面已经说过，精神与物质是否可以分开，已大是问题，精神离开物质，实无所谓精神，物质若离开精神，物质亦是死的，不能成其所以为文化现象。我们要知道，人类文化高下之分，是完全以物质的进步（即对自然的控制），为标准的。所谓石器时代、铜器时代、铁器时代，所谓文明与野蛮之分，精神方面是完全不计算在内的，因为精神文化是跟着物质的进步（即对自然的控制）为标准的，精神文化是跟着物质而进步的。未有不能控制自然而有高超精神之表现者，纵使有之，亦不过凝愚之无知而已。不然者，青羊宫道士的精神文化，可较爱因斯坦的为高，因其怡然自得，荣辱无萦于心的情况，远较孜孜不辍欲求探得宇宙之谜的爱因斯坦，相去诚不知几许。

然则青羊宫道士表现之精神为高乎？抑爱因斯坦表现之精神为高乎？此只能让读者自去下断议了！不过我们须记着，猴子所表现的精神态度，实远较人类者为佳。

此并非文化的唯物观，实为物质必藉精神以控制，精神必藉物质以表现，高超的精神文化，若无高超的物质文化以表现之，并不是真精神，而是无知，不然，未脱离旧石器时代之澳洲黑土人，亦可自称其精神文化较中国人或欧美之白人精神文化为高，而我们亦无从判断其优劣了。甘地之绝食，岂不是东方精神文化之最高的杰作，但在西方人看来，实幼稚、可笑。

东西文化建筑在共同基础之上

所有世界人类的文化，均建立在一原始文化基础之上，这是人类学上所共认的事实。所以魏士勒有"普遍文化型"的假设。虽然有人曾批评他实际上无所谓普遍的文化型，不过为一种普遍的需要，人类若要生存，则必须加以满足的。但无论如何，人类文化之共同基础，是不可否认的。

我们若缩小范围，只论旧大陆的东方与西方文化，其共同之文化基础，则更为显明，此一层，汉学家兼人类学家劳佛尔早已言之。例如支持旧世界文化之农业技能、家畜、车轮、社会组织、宗教观念等等，其基本之概念，实无不相同。其所不同者，不过因隔离及适应不同环境发生的枝枝叶叶而已。又如我们若执于了解西洋文化之西人而问之曰：西洋文化中最基本之发明为何？彼必曰纸张、印刷与火药三者。因为纸张与印刷之发明，使知识得以普及，科学得以迅速的发展。火药之发明，使欧人在军事上因之在政治上能处于优越之地位。然而此三种发明，皆中国人之发明也。那末，我们可以谓西洋文化为中国文化吗？西人必将掩口窃笑，我们也必将怒目而视，以为非我族类。

不过由此可以使我们能够看出东西文化的基础是基本相同的，换句话说，人类的文化，不问其古往今来，都是互相影响的，其中的交流，是继续不断的。未有一种文化完全与其他的文化隔离，而能发育孳长者。现在我们已牵连到文化上的另一个问题，即文化传播的问题。

文化的发展靠传播

若是树上的果子能够自动的落在我们口中的话，我想人类绝不会去发明用一根棍子将它搞下来，"怕麻烦"与"偷懒"恐怕是人类共有的天性罢，此或者是文化传播论者轻视人类发明天才的原因罢！但纵观人类文化史，发明的确是少见的现象。人类为解决自己的困难，凡能模仿他人类方法的时候，他决去模仿，而不自行发明。因此，若是一种文化专靠其本身力量以谋进步，纵然可以进步，亦是极慢的。澳大利亚的黑土人与北冰洋的亚斯基摩人，并非他们自甘于文化之落后，或智力之不如人，实因为他们处于边远的地带，外来的文化传不到他们当中罢了。我们若是将我们时常自诩为有五千年历史及东方文化的代表中国文化来分析一下，将中国人自己发明者留下，从外面传来者提出，那末，中国文化恐怕要倒退一万年，退入旧石器时代之中去了。如其不信，我们可将中国文化之基本支持者，农业中之发明加以分析就知道了。量近如玉黍蜀番薯的重要农作物，是近三百年或数十年间传入中国的，不用说了。以种植最早的五谷而言，若打开农业植物史一看，可以说没有一种是中国人首先发现或种植的。又以六畜而言，亦均非中国人首先驯养的（豕或可除外）又中国农作方法，以犁耕为基本，而犁则为近东埃及发明，其传入中国，大概是春秋战国之际。中国不是以农立国吗？而农业上的发明既已如此，若将其他外来文化特征除去，其不退入旧石器时代何也？此不独中国如此，而世界上的任何文化均莫不如此，其文化中的特征为其本国所自行发明者，十常不得一二。所以说，文化的发展与孳育，几全仗其吸收外来文化的能力，与夫外来的文化，能否传播到它的当中。我们若将东西文化细加分析，其中之重要特征，以为共有之基础，或为一方所发明而互相传播者，数量上实占大多数，在此种情形下，我们实际上只可谈文化的传播，还能谈什么东西文化？人类文化是一整个的，随便那一个民族的发明，其他任何民族均可得而利用之，问题是看它愿不愿意接受就是了！

　　我们若明白文化发展靠传播这一点，中国文化之接受西洋文化一层，自不成问题，而东西文化之讨论，亦思过半矣。

[原载《东方文化》第一卷第二期（1943 年）]

文化的决定性与个人

　　现在之研究文化者，不是过于注重文化的社会现象，即是偏重文化的心理现象。过于注重文化之社会现象者，以为文化是超个人的，是超生机的。个人有生有灭，而文化则是累积的、绵延的，及日趋于繁富的。个人之在于文化之中，直等于沧海之一粟，九牛之一毛，其生也文化不因之而增丰富，其灭也文化亦不因之而削弱。即人类中最大之发明家，其对于个人之供献亦不过等于千万分中之一而已，即以一此渺小之贡献而言，亦为文化之产物，完全受文化推动力之支配而不能自己，使其不得不从事于发明，即使无此类发明家，亦必有其他之发明家起而代之。反过来说，倘若文化未曾达到某一进程，即使有所发明，此类发明亦必归于湮没，对文化之进程上，亦不发生影响。譬如说，在公元前二世纪时 Hero of Alexandria 曾发明了一种蒸汽机，名叫 Aeolipile，其制为一圆球，有两管在球之正中互相顺延弯曲，球中贯以轴管，管有孔过于圆球之中，轴管两端向下弯曲通于锅炉之中，锅中贮水，炉下置火，火蒸汽发由轴管直入于圆球之中，继入球之弯曲管，乃夺管而出，球亦随之自动旋转。此种Aeolipile自原理上言之，实为一种反动力轮机（Reaction turbine）。然而Hero的Aeolipile超出了它的文化进程之前二千多年，纵然在当时发明了，亦无法加以利用，其结果只有归于湮没的一途，对于当时的文化，毫未发生印象。

再如文化之进程若达到某一阶级，其中必须有之发明，无论其有无某一个人，亦必需发明。以进化论而言，进化的思想，在西腊哲学家中即有之，其后经过罗马时代，以及中世纪，哲学家时之有加以申论的，诗人亦时有加以歌颂的，但对于思想学术上毫未发生影响。在十八及十九世纪之交，各经过劳马克之功用论的解释，但学术之进步，倘未达到接受之时期，故不只不能发生效果，反为人所抑揄，其后生物学之进步，及地质学上之进步，特别为Hunon及Lyell之倡导渐趋于一致论（Uniformitarianism）的解释，故在一八五九年达尔文的物种原始出之后，即能风靡一世，人类思想中掀起了一大革命，无有一种学术不受它的影响，说者以十九世纪为进化论的世纪，亦并非过词。不过进化论的思想之所以能如此的，当然要归功于达尔文的物竞天择优胜劣败的解释，以及其引证之详明，文章之典雅，几使阅者不能不动摇于中，对其论证加以考虑，但是若是文化的进程尚未达到接受的阶段，虽有达尔文的物种原始，不只文不能为功，恐怕它的命运亦要与Hero的Aeolipile相同了。所以说进化论的思想，所以能如此的，固然要归功于达尔文，但是在十九世纪中叶，人类文化的进程，已经是不能不有进化论的思想，为之维系，故无论有无达尔文，物竞天择之进化解释终需出现，达尔文亦不过适逢其会罢了。要之，达尔文亦是文化之产物，而不能超出文化之上，我们岂不闻与达尔文各不相谋而达到同样的结论的，岂不尚有瓦勒斯吗？所以说文化的进程已经达到要进化观念的必要，倘无达尔文，尚有瓦勒斯，纵无瓦勒斯，亦必有其他之一个人起而代之，达尔文瓦勒斯岂能超出文化的进程以外吗？孟德尔的遗传律的发现，岂不更为明显。孟德尔[有]关遗传研究论文的发表，是在一八六六年，但在当时毫未有人加以注意，过了三十余年后，在一九〇〇年荷兰之 De Vries 德国之 Correns 奥国之 Tschermak，三人在毫不知道孟德尔的研究及论文之下，根据各人之独立，对于遗传的研究，而得了与孟德尔同样的结果，因为 De Vries 等三人的研究，人们才注意到三十余年前的孟德尔的论文，而奉之为开山祖师，孟德尔的遗传公式，不只成了生物遗传上的一定不移的定理，而成了一独立的科学遗传化学（Genetics）。若有人试问何以孟德尔[的遗传]律发表之初，未有人加以注意，直等到三数十年后方觉其贡献之大？此实亦显而易见。因为达尔文的物种原始方发表未久（七年以前发表），生物的研究上尚无此种需要，故虽有人发现，而亦等于不发现。等到十九世纪终了，二十世纪开始时，生物学的研究上，又对于物竞天择之学说上已有一种遗传律的需要，故 De Vries 等各不相谋的同时加以重新发现，文化的超个人性岂不更为明显吗？所以，马可尼若生于马克斯威尔（Maxwell）之前，决不会发明无线电报，换句话说，就是没有马可尼，我们今日还是有无线[电]报用。文化的进展，决不会因为没有马可尼，而决定其有没有无线电报，因为电磁学的研究，自马克斯威尔以来，已经为无线电报的发明，立下了以需的基础，故到马可尼之时，纵无马可尼其个人，他人亦必起而发明之。我们若将人类发明史翻出来一看，其中的许多最重要的发明，多不是经多人各不相谋的独立发明吗？爱克司光及人类中血型（Bloodgroups）的发现，岂不是最好的明证吗？所以说，文化的进展，是超乎个人之上的，超乎生机之上的（Superorganic）。爱因斯坦若生于数目上数不清五个单位的原始民族之中，他终身的努力，决不会超出十进数范围之外，岂能发明相对论吗？

在注重文化之心理方面者看来，以为无论哪一种文化的成分，若将其寻根溯源，细加分析，无有不归根到个人的。人类文化中宁有无发明家的发明么？不过有若干最古而最重要的发明或发现，它们的发明或发现者，因时代过久，失于年代缥缈之中，无纵稽考罢了。但无论哪一种文化的成分，其曾经过一度的发明或发现，那是无可疑问的。所以说文化的根源，还是个人，个人是文化的担负者、传递者、承继者，舍去文化的根源之心理的个人，而高谈文化的超个人性，直等于缘木而求鱼了。更有若干社会学家，提出所谓集体心灵（Collective mind）或集体知觉（Collective Consciousness）等标题，以实证文化的超个人性，是不过在知识上欲求一终南捷径，对于文化的认识上，是无所裨益的。所以说，我们不要认识文化则已，倘若我们要正确认识文化，则必须同时认到文化的个人根源。

这两种见解，各有所偏，而未能以窥文化之全面。文化是有它的相当的超个人性，换言之，即其决定性，倘若一种文化没有它的决定性，那一种文化就根本不能继续、不能存在。因为一种文化所以能永远的自续而不绝者，正因为能决定它那一文化中的每一个人的行为，合乎它那一文化的既定模型，而成文化中的有力担负份子。不过文化之实在性的表现，终是个人。文化的泉源，及文化能否前进发展，亦端靠其中的个人之天才、能力、及活动的精力如何？倘若没有个人，就根本没有文化了，二者是互为因果的。现在有一个比譬，主张文化之超个人论者，可以说只见到森林，而未见到一根一根的树木；注重文化中之心理现象者，只见到一根一根的树木，而未看见森林。当然，文化与个人的关系，不是如此简单的，因为文化的现象是不能估量或捉摸的，所以研究文化的人，好像一个研究原子的物理学家一样，不能直接观察它的实在性与实质，只能从它所产生的结果以推测之。不过，森林与树木的譬喻，亦可见其各偏重一方面的情况。

我们若要明瞭文化与个人的关系，我们必需先知道自生物学上看来，人类不是一种野生动物而是一种家生动物。人类之所以成为家生的，即是他曾经受过文化的驯养。换句话说，"人"根本是一个文化的动物。人若离开文化，就根本不能成其所以为人，人也就根本离不开文化。我们人类自呱呱坠地之时，并不是诞生在一个毫无人烟的荒岛之上，而是诞生在一个已有数十万年甚至数百万年的历史的文化集团之中。每一个人自从他诞生之时起，及至生长成熟而至于老死，他的一呼一息、一举一动，无不受他所诞生文化中的影响。他的习惯、思想、举动、言行，凡一切行为，无不受他所诞生中的文化的熏陶，不能脱乎他那一文化的模型。这在个人方面，是无可逃避的，必需受文化的驯养的。而文化的工用，亦即在此，训练一代一代的个人，以继续文化的活动，使每一个人的行为，合乎他那一文化的定型。在一方面，使他可以应付自然环境；在另一方面，而且是最重要的一方面，使他在他那一文化系统中得到一适[当]的地位，换句话说，即是如何的应付社会。因为每一个人的生活在文化之中，应付自然环境则比较容易，而应付社会中的其他个人，实比较困难。而一种文化的功能效率如何，亦以此为征验了。

自表面上看来，文化确能超出个人而永存不灭。其所以能如此者，其一方面，因其能训练一代一代的个人以继续文化的活动，因此其中个人的一切行为，无论其如何奔放不羁，总不能超出其文化定型以外。在另一方面，因为担负整个文化活动者，并非单独隔离之个人，乃系集团，因为人类文化之繁复，无论个人之天才如何，绝不是个人能力加以全部习学的，并且亦不需要。我们常说周公、孔子集中国文化之大成，然而周公、孔子之所知者，亦不过中国当时的哲学、文学、宗教，以及所谓礼、乐、射、御、书、教齐家治国天下之大端而已，至于稼穑、铸剑、牧马，以及其他种种之工艺，必为其所不知，故樊迟问学稼，孔子则答之曰，吾不如老农老圃，然而种田之知识在中国文化中的地位，在我们现在看来，自不亚于哲学或宗教，或且还要超过之。

　　所以在任何一种文化之中，即使在最简单的原始文化当中，未有一个人能将其全部加以学习者，或能通晓其全部者。此乃不可能之事，亦且不必。例如农人可利用铁制农具，而不必通晓矿工及铁工之事。著作家可将其作品印刷成书，至对于排版、印刷、铸字、造纸，以及一切关于印书之必要先决条件，虽一无所知，亦无关重要。一社会中每一份子之所以需要通晓者，不过其文化中之一部分，或数部分，使其在整个文化之中，得其应得之适当地位。文化对于个人之重要功能，就在于此了。

　　担负一整个文化者，既为多数个人集合之集团，此集团之中，包涵将要过去之老人，正在担负文化活动之壮年及正在训练中而为将来担负文化活动之青年及幼童，这种集团在生物上系一种自动继续的机构，除非经过特殊外界的干涉之外，是不会毁灭的。故文化亦随之而自动继续，担负文化的集团永远存在，其所担负之文化即永远存在。所以说并不是超生机的，而是建立在有生机的及有生灵的个人之上集团文化，不能离开生机，不能离开个人而独立存在。生物的集团何以能自续？从生物学上讲，机生侯体（Organism）是不灭的，韦思曼（Weismann）的有名的遗传素之永远继续（Continuity of the germ-plasm）说，即是此意。据韦思曼之说，由这一代发生下一代之遗传素，对于其发展其中的父母体是独立的，故多细胞的生机体有死亡，而卵细胞（Germ-cell）仍是继续的发生下一代，故韦思曼曾指出，卵细胞是永生而不死亡的。故地球上自有生物以来，个体的死亡，并未阻生命的发展与继续，即是如此。

　　社会的集团的构成是在生物中有心灵的个人，而生命的永远的继续，是在于独立绵延的遗传素。生命既是永远的衔接而不间断，建在生命机构之上的社会集体及文化，亦因之永远不会间断，只要人类一天存在，文化即一天存在。离开生物的基础而高谈文化是超个人的，是超生机的，以致文化的本质，愈弄愈不明白，而愈玄妙了。马兰劳斯基因为反对 Durkheim 集体心灵之说，而以为文化之超个人性系由于物质文化之相因与连续，然而他实不知，物质文化之相因与继续，亦系基于生理的反心理的个人，若离开个人，物质文化，还是死的，而不能自行继续。

　　至于文化何以有其固定性？个人何以不能离开文化的模型？这种关系，从下面一个例子更可以明瞭。研究文化现象的，时常感到文化这现象到底有没有这种东西？或者是研究者的心目中的一种抽象作用，在实质上是感觉不到的。文化是否有实质？或有一种特征？是不能直接观察，或直接感觉的。就是生活在那一种文化当中的个人，亦不知其有文化这种东西。我们若要看到一种文化的实现，当在那一种文化以外的行为求之。譬如我们生长汉地，我们中国文化的特点，谁也不感觉其特异，但是我们一到边地，就可以感觉到中国文化的实在性了，凡边地有汉人聚居的地方，汉人的文化亦随之而往，所有的建筑、衣饰、习惯、语言，无不与内地相同，而四周则为完全不同的夷人文化所包围，汉人文化好像一大海中孤峰独起，为愈显得它的真实性与特异性。又如在美国各大城市中有汉人聚居的地方，美国人称之曰中国城，因其文化表现完全为汉式，而与四周的欧美文化不同的缘故。我们要问，国人何以要如此？为什么到了一种完全不同的文化环境之中，不能随之俱化，反而要表现其固有文化的这问题？显而易见，因为文化的担负者是个人，而个人受了他生长中的文化训练、熏陶、习染，其生理上的肌肉动作习惯，已经养成，后来虽然到了一种不同的文化习惯之中，亦不能轻易随之俱化，总是要回到他已经自小养成的动作习惯，因为此种动作习惯对于他为最容易，为最省力。好比我们的汉语习惯已经养成之后，若学英语或德语，总脱不了一种汉语的腔调，无论如何，总不觉得如说汉语来得方便，这完全是因为语言动作已经养成的缘故。所以说因为文化的行为系基于个人生理上的关系，所以才有它的实在性及固定性，虽然它在表面上好像表现一种超个人性或超生机性的形态，其实是离不开个人的，离开个人，文化就消灭了。一种文化，只要它当中的最后一人存在，那种文化即算存在，此最后的一人死亡，那种文化就随之而灭亡了。在民族学中，时常能从一种文化的最后一人得到那种文化的梗概，即是如此。而个人呢，因为自诞生后即受他那一种文化的训练熏陶，迨其肌肉动作习惯一经养成之后，在他的一生之中，永远跳不出他那一种文化范畴之外，不只他一生跳不出他所诞生中的文化圈套之外，而他在无形及不知不觉之中，反要训练下一代亦作此种动作，而不能自己。

无论那一种文化，都有它的决定性，若是一种文化没于文化没有它的自行决定性，而可以随便变动，那就根本不能成为一种文化，因为一种文化的机构若可以随便变动，那就不能保持它的特质。一种文化倘不能自保其特质，那还成为一种文化吗？那末，个人在文化的决定性之下，是毫无自由的吗？或完全是文化的奴隶吗？是又不尽然。我们要知道，一种文化虽恃其决定性以保持其固有的特质及自续性，然而文化并不是永远不变的，无论那一种文化，都是时时在那里生长及变动，不过这种生长或变动一样，是在不知不觉之中，在短期内其中个人所自觉的。即以我们的中国文化而论，普通一般人，以为中国从古至今是一贯的，它的当中是没有什么大的变动。在从前，不只中国的一般学者如此着想，即是外人习于文化变动而来研究中国文化的，亦抱着此种观念。不过这实在是错误的，中国文化，不只在生长变动，而且变动得很大。殷周以前的文化，用不着说了，若是我们能起汉代的人于今日中国社会之中大半的人们，决不承认他是同一文化的中国人，不只他说的话，我们听不大懂，他的一切的生活习性与我们都不一样，然而现在我们尚在自称是他的嫡系苗裔呢！或者诸位，以为我的如此说法为太过一点，那末别的不用提了，即以成都附近以及新津、彭山、嘉定而下至叙府的汉代崖墓而言，即依山凿石的汉代墓葬，当地的土人，称它为什么……他们并不称它为汉人祖先的墓葬，或甚至与汉人有关的东西，而称之曰蛮子洞，因其他们决不想到他们的祖先会如此的。即此一端即可见，中国文化自汉以来变动之大，而遑论殷周了。

随便哪一种文化，都是当时在那里不知不觉的生长和变动，换句话说，即在向前演进。在此种生长变动之中，个人的功能，就觉其重要了。前面已经讲过，文化的主要功能，在训练它当中的一代一代的个人合乎那一种文化的型范，在各种行动上能表现一致。我们个人生来是没有固定的性格的，个人性格的养成，是看他所在的文化上的型范如何，文化的功能，在使其中的每一个人的性格，都合乎该文化的型范。但在同一文化中的个人性格的养成，虽在大体彼此相同，但其中不能不有个别的差异，譬如与一种生物继续一样，一代与一代间的个体，靠着遗传的力量虽然相似，但每一个体之间，总不能完全相同，而有相当的变异，这种变易的累积，据进化的理论，就是物种的原始了。在文化中个人性格的变易之累积，亦就是各种不同的文化特征的原始了。

文化的本身是不能思想或动作的，而它的思想与动作的表现，完全要靠着个人，而个人的性格表现于思想与行为上者，虽能与文化固定型范一致，但其中每有不少的变异，此类变异的累积，其结果可与原来的定型完全不同，所以个人的行为在文化的定型范畴以内，有他的自由，而不受限制的。我们时常称某人的行为放荡不羁、滑稽玩世，以近代术语出之，所谓不羁、玩世，就是他的行为超出那种文化的定型之外，而与其他个人行为不一致之谓。文化及社会对于这种玩世不羁的行为的容忍性，在各文化中各有不同，有者容耐性甚大，有者即根本不容其存在，但无论如何，此等所谓"生性孤僻，不合时宜"的个人，在其一生中的境遇中必到处坎坷，为社会所不容。倘若他要在社会上有所建树，则必须一变其玩世不羁的行为，与文化的定型相合，方能有所成就。然文化的猛进，亦有时靠此种不羁的个人。这种例子，在历史上不知有多少，此处亦不必赘举了。

无论文化的哪一种新特征，不管他是属于物质的或属于精神的无不发源于个人的变异（此处所谓变异，包括发明与发现，因为发明与发现，只系根据旧有之材料，而变为一种新东西而已）。个人时常在那里想变新花样，时时在那里想换一换新环境，恶单调而喜新异，或者是人类共有的特征罢！这种个人欢喜新异的趋向，乃是人类文化能向前进步的一种大原动力。我们若将人类发明史翻出来一看，许多重要的发明，并不只发明一次，有的不知先后发明了若干次，有的系在极恶劣的文化反压力之下发明的，此足以反证个人不完全是文化的奴隶，不完全受文化的支配。公元前二世纪，希腊及埃及的文化，并不需要蒸汽机，而Hero偏要发明Aeolipile，哥伯尼在举世为地球中心说笼罩之下而发现地球绕日运行，与当时之文化的信条相反，加里尼欧偏要宣传此种学说，结果经教廷之压迫，不能不自承认其错误，如今则成为天文学中一定不移之真理了。劳马克与赫顿在特别创造说与灾变论风靡一世时之际，一则主张生物的进化，一则主张地质的进化，与当时的信条大相违反，结果为当时的社会所抑揄所唾骂。来尔竟叛其师说，而在他的名著《地质学原理》中倡导地质演化一致论。达尔文在其《物种原始》之中，尚不敢明言人类系从低等物种进化而来，因为他恐怕因此引起误会，以致影响他的生物进化学说的接受。孟德尔在举世不注意遗传之时，而偏要发现他的遗传律。由此可以明白个人并不完全受文化的范畴，个人中实不乏文化的叛徒，往往与训练他的文化，走上相反的途程。其结果，文化亦往往因一两个人而改观，所以说，文化是个人所得的遗传来的资本，而如何利用这遗传下来的资本，则在乎个人了。有者守着这一点资本，不敢越雷池一步，作为他一生受用不尽的宝藏。有者则利用这种资本，作为新事业的根基。前者为普通一般人，后者即我们当中的发明家。

文化之决定性弱者，对于个人之变异，任之自然，而不加制止；文化之决定性强者，对于个人之变异，往往不能容忍，必须压制之，或消灭之而后已。我们若问哪一种文化，对于变异之接受为易、其演变为速？这一个问题，当然不易答复，因为我们对于各个文化发展的历史，知道得不很详细，而所知道的期间，亦太短促，不足以归纳成一定理。不过所可言者，在决定性较弱之文化中，个人之变异，往往不能引起其他个人之意，因人人得而自动变异，则变异不足，炫为新奇，因之不能传给他人，不能成文化特征。反之，压迫愈大，愈成"其操心也危，其虑思也深"而促其创新的，亦非罕见之事。故曰文化有决定性，个人亦有发明与发现的自由。

[原载《华文月刊》第一卷第四期（1942 年）]

CHINESE MYTHOLOGY AND DR. FERGUSON

Before criticizing adversely a scholar's work, two things should be ascertained with reasonable certainty: first, is the work to be criticized of sufficient importance to justify attention; and second, are the errors of the book so misleading as to call for correction.

A series of thirteen volumes, entitled *The Mythology of All Races*, has been issued by the Archaeological Institute of America, under the editorship of Canon J. A. MacCulloch and the late Professor G. F. Moore. Volume VIII, published in 1928, contains *Chinese*, by John C. Ferguson, and *Japanese,* by Masaharu Anesaki. It is with the work of Dr. Ferguson that this article is primarily concerned.

It is evident from the learned society which has issued these volumes, from the reputation of the editors, and from the names of the well known specialists who have written the other volumes, that this series is intended to be authoritative. Both Ferguson and Anesaki are well known scholars. The former has long been considered an authority on Chinese art, and it is generally understood that he is widely read in Chinese literature and has been closely connected with Chinese official and scholarly circles. Under such circumstances, if his work should be shown to contain careless generalizations, faulty classification, and misstatements of fact, it is a very serious matter. Scholars in other fields should have confidence that in relying upon statements made in such a work they are upon firm ground, and sinologists should be able to feel that this ground need not be gone over again.

It may be said at once that from a scholarly standpoint, the work of Ferguson is inferior to that of Anesaki. For example, the latter has provided notes in which he explains etymologies, elaborates difficult points, and gives exact references to his sources. On the other hand, Ferguson refers to an impressive array of Chinese works, but by omitting exact references, makes it practically impossible for a western scholar to check him with any thoroughness.

This is especially clear in his concluding chapter on "Criticism," in which he considers only two men, Wang T'ung and Han Yü. His choice of

Wang T'ung and Han Yü is regretable. Wang T'ung has sometimes been regarded as a myth himself, but there are two existing books attributed to him, the *Wên chung tzǔ chung shuo* and the *Yüan ching*. There is nothing in them which can be interpreted as a criticism of Chinese myths, although there is some criticism of older literature on other grounds, and both books have been considered forgeries. Han Yü is mentioned as a critic because of his essays on the bone of the Buddha and to the crocodile. The former has nothing to do with the questions of mythology, simply reflecting the opposition of orthodox Confucians to Buddhism, while the latter is probably a sincere appeal to the crocodile. Such matter is not myth in the sense in which ethnologists use the word.

Dr. Ferguson is also uncritical in his use and selection of sources. Many of the works he cites are simply books of fiction, and no one would consider Frankenstein and Dracula to be myths of the English people. He devotes a chapter to "Theatrical Tales"; but while the Chinese drama does sometimes deal with mythology, the myths are so changed for theatrical purposes as to make the drama of little use in a serious study of mythology.

He does not account for the historical development of his myths. This point may be illustrated by a figure whom Dr. Ferguson treats in some detail (pp. 116-118), Hsi Wang Mu, but as if the conception of the goddess were entirely static. Now in the oldest sections of the *Shan hai ching*, the "*Hsi shan ching*" and the "*Hai nei pei ching*," Hsi Wang Mu has a human body with a leopard's tail and tiger's teeth, is fond of whistling, has dishevelled hair, wears jade ornaments, and eats three black-birds. The deity presides over plague, and the sex is not indicated. In the "*Ta huang hsi ching,*" the divinity lives in a cave, and is dreadful in appearance. In a later work, the *Mu t'ien tzǔ chuan*, the goddess has dropped her animal attributes and is an educated Chinese queen.[1] In *Huai nan tzǔ*, written about 100 B.C., she no longer presides over pestilence, but has become the goddess possessing the elixir of immortality.[2] Finally, in the *Han Wu Ti nei chuan*,[3] the goddess reaches her full state, living in heavenly palaces with courtiers in an establishment modelled on the court of the Han emperors. Dr. Ferguson gives no account whatever of this development, which would be essential in a critical study.

In the "Introduction", Dr. Ferguson over simplifies Chinese culture. That he divides it into Confucian and Taoist spheres is not so bad, even though to do so ignores other important influences. But he goes further and identifies Confucianism with conservatism characterized by ceremonialism, and Taoism with liberalism typified by divination. Such an association is incorrect, because both ceremonialism and divination are characteristic of Confucianism and neither of them is characteristic of Taoism. He says that the Liberal School adhered "to the Eight Diagrams reputed to have been

---

[1] *Mu t'ien tzǔ chuan*, bk. 3.

[2] *Huai nan hung lieh chi chieh* (淮南鸿烈集解),Shanghai,c.p.,1922, Bk. 6, p. 16.

[3] A forgery attributed to Pan Ku, but the date of its compilation cannot be later than the third and fourth centuries.

西王母

Hsi Wang Mu as described in the *Shan hai ching* From the Collection of the Chinese Library, Harvard University

Hsi Wang Mu as illustrated in the *Hsien fu ch'i tsung* From the Collection of the Chinese Library, Harvard University

evolved by Fu Hsi from the marks found on the back of a dragon horse," and found its ancient authorization in the *Book of Changes* (p. 8). But the story of the Eight Diagrams of Fu Hsi is the Confucian myth of the invention of writing. Lao Tzǔ does not mention the *Book of Changes*, but it was spoken of in the highest terms by Confucius.[1] It is, indeed, one of the most

---

[1] "Given a few more years of life to finish my study of the *Book of Changes*, I may be free from great errors." *Analects*, VII, 16. This passage is sometimes questioned, but it is the generally accepted version.

important canons of Confucianism. [1]

By saying that the Liberal School "provides for changes amidst changing circumstances"(p. 8), Dr. Ferguson misinterprets the positions of *I Yin, T'ai Kung, Yü Hsiung and Kuan Chung* [2] (p. 9), and by confusing the adepts and legalists with the Taoist philosophers,[3] he calls Ch'in Shih Huang "the greatest supporter of Liberalism..."(p. 9).

The "Introduction" closes with an account of the story of K'ung An kuo and his labors on the text of the *Analects* and the *Spring and Autumn Annals*.

"During the Han dynasty, about 150 B.C., the sayings of Confucius were compiled by one of his descendants, K'ung An-kuo. This compilation, called *Lun yü hsün tz'ü*, was based upon the comparison of two texts. One of these was found with other texts, *pi chung shu*, in

---

[1] It was the priests of the Taoist religion (which is of much later origin), who utilized the *na-chia* method of the commentators of the Later Han dynasty on the *Book of Changes* in the practice of alchemy and the manufacture of the elixir of life, which has nothing to do with Taoism as a school of philosophy.

[2] Dr. Ferguson alludes (p. 9) to I Yin advising T'ang to plot against Hsia, T'ai Kung and Yü Hsiung advising Wên Wang and Wu Wang against Shang, and Kuan Chung "the first to make a feudal state assume hegemony among other states" as "authoritative examples of the early Tao." But I Yin was one of the most important heroes of Confucianism and is ranked as high as Chou Kung. Ch'êng T'ang, Wên Wang and Wu Wang, whom I Yin, T'ai Kung and Yü Hsiung advised, were the model emperors of Confucianism, and their revolutions against the existing regimes were highly commended and justified by the most orthodox Confucianists. These legendary figures do not prove the liberalism of Taoism, nor do they prove the conservatism of Confucianism. Kuan Chung's writings (those attributed to him) are decidedly legal in nature and they have been classed under the School of Law since the *Han shu i wen chih* (Bibliographical section of the History of the Former Han dynasty).

[3] The adepts, or magicians, should be sharply distinguished from the Taoist philosophers.

a wall of the home of Confucius when it was being demolished by Kung Wang, son of the Emperor Ching Ti, who was appointed by his father to be King of the Principality of Lu (modern Shangtung). This text was written in the so called 'tadpole' characters, *k'o-tou-wên*, and is known as the 'ancient text,' *ku wên*. The other text came from the neighbouring principality of Ch'i and, being written in the characters which were used in the last years of the Chow dynasty, is known as the 'modern text,' *chin wên*. The compilation of K'ung An kuo, with some emendations, has remained the standard of the Conservative School for all succeeding generations, and as it includes the *Ch'un Ch'iu* , or '*Spring and Autumn Annals*,' it carries back the account of China's ancient civilization to a great antiquity." (pp. 10 11)

What evidence is there that K'ung An-kuo made a compilation of two texts of the *Analects* and included in it the *Annals*, which he called the *Lun yü hsün tz'ŭ* ?[1] In what bibliography is this work to be found?[2] It is said in a work by Ho Yen[3] and in *Sui-shu ching chi chih* that K'ung An-kuo wrote a commentary on the *Ku lun yü*, but they say nothing of the comparison with the Ch'i text and its inclusion in the *Ch'un ch'iu*. Even these references are

---

[1]　No such work is known.

[2]　The *Han shu i wen chih* is the earliest of the Chinese bibliographies existant and is used as a comprehensive checklist of ancient Chinese literature. It says nothing of the compilation of K'ung An-kuo.

[3]　In the preface of the *Lun yü chi chieh* , a work compiled under the editorship of Ho Yen.

doubtful. If this is meant to be the compilation of K'ung An-kuo, it did not remain the "standard of the Conservative School for all succeeding generations," because it was said to have been lost by Ho Yen himself. No attempt to combine these two books was ever made, and they cannot carry back the "account of China's ancient civilization to a great antiquity," because the *Lun yü* consists of the sayings of Confucius collected together by his disciples and the *Ch'un Ch'iu* is a history of the period 722-481 B.C. in outline form.

In the chapter on "Taoism" Dr. Ferguson continually confuses Taoism as a philosophy with Taoism as a religion. The latter was founded by Chang Tao-ling and its philosophical foundation was laid by Ko Hung more than a century later. Ko Hung was Confucian in ethics though Taoist in metaphysics, and opposed the naturalism of Lao Tzŭ. Lao Tzŭ was a monistic philosopher with no belief in a personal God, and it is one of the ironies of history that centuries later he was deified, and regarded as the founder of a religion. As an example of the inaccuracy of this chapter it may be noticed that T'ang T'ai Tsung is said first to have claimed descent from Lao Tzŭ (p. 14), and to have given the sage the title of Hsüau Yüan Huang Ti (p. 22). The first of these acts was performed by T'ang Kao Tsu,[1] and the second by T'ang Kao

---

[1] According to *Fêng shih Wên chien chi* (Book l, first section, Taoist religion), in the third year of Wu Tê (620 A.D.) of the Emperor Kao Tsu, Chi Shan-hsing of Chin-chou saw an old man clad in white on the Yangchio mountains, who called to him and said: "Tell the Emperor of T'ang, that I am Lao Chün and that I am your ancestor. There will be no bandits this year and there will be peace." Kao Tsu immediately sent an envoy who offered a sacrifice to Lao Tzŭ and built a temple to him on the site of the revelation, and changed the name of

Tsung, ① neither being the act of T'ai Tsung.

At the end of this chapter (p. 24), Dr. Ferguson says, "The relation of Taoism to the mythological characters of China... is complete. If we were to depend upon the views of the School of Letters (Confucian) we should have scant material." In chapter III, the chief characters considered are Yao, Shun, Yü, T'ang, Wên and Wu, but far from being connected with Taoism, these men are the heroes of the Confucian canon. Indeed, throughout the whole book Dr. Ferguson quotes more from Confucian than from Taoist works.

As a matter of fact, it would be a mistake to attempt an account of Chinese mythology solely from either Confucian or Taoist sources. In the Confucian canon there are probably many myths, but most of them have been so rationalized that they can be discovered only with the aid of other sources. As for the religious books of Taoism, they are all late, and nearly all their gods are of relatively recent date. Where the Taoist gods are connected with myths, they must be examined very carefully in order to discover the original form. Late Taoist literature is full of legendary inventions, but is not of great value in the study of ancient Chinese folklore and mythology. It would seem as if Dr. Ferguson has made the same mistake

---

the district Fu-shan to Shên-shan, "mountain of god." Kao-tsu (618-626 A.D.) was T'ai Tsung's father. T'ai Tsung ruled from 627-649 A.D.

① The canonization of Lao-tzü as Hsüan Yüan Huang Ti, according to both *the Old and New T'ang Histories*, was in the first year of Ch'ien Fêng (666 A.D.) of the Emperor Kao Tsung. This was sixteen years after the death of T'ai Tsung.

as Werner,[1] and considered such works as the *Shên hsien t'ung chien*[2] as mythology, whereas they are mainly deliberate inventions.

In the chapter on "Cosmogony," Dr. Ferguson gives an account of the metaphysical speculations of the Taoist philosophers, which are not myths at all. After referring to the story of P'an Ku as an importation from Siam,[3] he devotes some space to Yü Huang, the "Pearly Emperor." Here (p. 59), Dr. Ferguson says, "This is the first appearance of yü Huang" (and adds that absolutely nothing is known of his origin or life), referring to a story in the *T'ung chien kang mu* of a dream of Sung Chên Tsung, and gives an account of his life from the *Sou shên chi.*[4] Dr. Ferguson has apparently followed

[1]　E. T. C. Werner, *Myths and Legends of China*, 1922.

[2]　A book of biographies chiefly of the Taoist gods, saints and sages, and in which is included a short life of Christ which was translated into English by E. T. C. Werner in the *Journal of the Royal Asiatic Society, North China Branch*, Vol. LII, pp. 186-191.

[3]　Perhaps a cosmogonic myth of the south that migrated northward. Where it originated is still undetermined. Dr. Ferguson referred to the book *Shu i chi* of the sixth century A.D., but the myth was recorded in a much earlier work, the *San wu li chi* by Hsü Chêng, of the third century A.D. It does not say definitely that the myth originated in Siam.

[4]　Whenever only the title *Sou shên chi* is referred to, it is always understood by scholars to be the well known work attributed to Kan Pao of the fourth century A.D. But the life of Yü Huang given by Dr. Ferguson is not to be found there. There is another secondary and obscure work of the same title but of much later compilation (compiled about the end of the sixteenth century A.D.) included in the *Tao tsang* (道藏). An account of the life of Yü Huang was given in the first book (pp. 9-10) of this work. But the matter is made more confusing in the case of Chiang Tzǔ-wên (p. 65) where Dr. Ferguson also simply referred to the *Sou shên chi*, because this story appears in both of these works. From the nature of the story given by Dr. Ferguson, it was apparently adapted from Kan Pao's work, although Dr. Ferguson's account does not follow either book accurately. But in the case of Yü Huang, it would be entirely wrong to assume the title to be Kan Pao's work because it was compiled at least four centuries before the time of the Sung emperor Chên Tsung, and it would be useless to refer to the work in the *Tao tsang* because it is not original and merely an adaptation from different sources. As a matter of fact, the life of Yü Huang appeared in a much earlier work, the *Kao shang yü huang pên hsing chi ching*, than the *Sou shên chi* of the *Tao tsang*.

Werner ① and made the same mistake. The name Yü Huang was much earlier than the time of the Emperor Chên Tsung, appearing in the writings of Han Yü (768-824 A.D.) whom Dr. Ferguson has chosen as one of the critics of Chinese myths, in Liu Tsung-yüan (773-819 A.D.) and in Yüan Chen (779-831 A.D.). All these men lived about two centuries before the time of Chên Tsung. It is apparent that the myth of Yü Huang was originated at least two or three centuries before Chên Tsung's time and reached its fullest development in the tenth century, for a vivid celestial court scene of Yü Huang was painted by the famous artist Shih K'o of the Later Shu Kingdom (908-965 A.D.), as recorded in the work of Li Chien, *Tê yü chai hua p'in*.② Most astonishing of all, Dr. Ferguson says (p. 55), "Liu Hsiang was the author of the *History of the Han Dynasty* and the founder of the modern style of historical composition." If Dr. Ferguson can produce a history of the Han written by Liu Hsiang, he has made a momentous discovery, but it is more likely that he wrote Liu Hsiang while intending to write Pan Ku. Liu Hsiang was a co-author of a bibliography which was one of the sources of the *Ch'ien han shu*.

The chapter on "Spirits of Nature" ought to be the heart of the book. Yet after mentioning some ceremonials, all taken from Confucian sources, Dr. Ferguson soon passes to the consideration of such deities as the Earth-

---

① E.T. C. Werner, *Myths and Legends of China*, pp. 130-131.
② 宋李廌撰德隅斋画品，顾氏文房小说本，pp.7-8.

Gods, the City-Gods, the "T'ien Hou," and other tutelary gods. Unfortunately these gods have little to do with nature myths.

Yet the Chinese possess a rich store of myths concerning the sun, moon, stars, clouds, mountains, rivers, and other natural objects, and one of these, ignored by Dr. Ferguson, may be taken briefly as an example. Hsi Ho was an ancient Chinese sun god, or charioteer of the sun. The earliest appearance of the name is in the "Canon of Yao" of the *History*, where the myth has been rationalized and Hsi Ho, whether a personal name or a title, is a sort of court astrologer. But in the *Shan hai ching* is a different account.

"Between the Southeastern Sea and the 'Sweet Water' is a land called Hsi Ho. There was a woman named Hsi Ho who bathed the sun in Kan Yen. She was the wife of Ti Chün [1] and gave birth to ten suns. " A commentator on this passage [2] considered that Hsi Ho was the one who took charge of the sun and moon at the beginning of the world. In *Chuang Tzǔ*[3] it is said that on one occasion ten suns appeared at once, which caused a general conflagration. This incident is still further developed in *Huai-nan Tzu*,[4] who places it in the time of Yao. Each sun contained a crow.[5] Yao ordered I to shoot the suns. I

---

[1] Literally Emperor Chün. He is an important figure in ancient Chinese mythology, and may be compared with Zeus as the head of the Chinese mythical hierarchy. Dr. Ferguson ignores him entirely.

[2] Kuo P'o, *Shan hai ching*, bk. 15, "Ta huang nan ching."

[3] *Chuang tzǔ*: 昔者十日并出，草木焦枯.

[4] *Huai nan hung lieh chi chieh*, bk. 8, "Pên ching hsün," pp. 7-8.

[5] The *Shan hai ching* says: "There is a crow in the sun."

shot nine, and the crows in them fell dead,[①] leaving the one sun which we still possess. This story explains the association of the crow with the sun. It would be interesting to speculate whether this story has any connection with the widely diffused myth of the thunder-bird.

In the *Li sao* there is a hint that Hsi Ho is the charioteer of the sun,[②] and *Huai-nan Tzu* says that the sun rides in a chariot drawn by six dragons driven by Hsi Ho. There is an account of the daily journey past different places which correspond to the daylight hours of the Chinese day.[③] Some of these names became the nuclei for later legends. The *Shan hai ching* contains legends about worthies who regulated the course of the sun,[④] and H*uai-nan Tzǔ* ascribes eclipses to the combats of unicorns.[⑤] The legend of the heavenly dog eating the sun and moon during eclipses is of late origin, and the custom of beating gongs to save them is said to have been introduced from India.

This brief account of the development of a sun myth illustrates the way in which Chinese myths should be treated, as well as the difficulties inherent in the material, for it will be seen that references must be collected from many sources.[⑥] It should be noticed that the *History* is supposed to be much

---

①   See *Ch'u tz'ü*, "Tien wên."

②   *Li sao*, tr. by Lim Boon keng, p. 81, XLVIII.

③   *Huai nan hung lieh chi chieh*, bk. 3, "T'ien wên hsün," pp. 18-19.

④   *Shan hai Ching*, Book 14, and 16.

⑤   *Huai nan hung lieh chi chieh*, bk. 3, "T'ien wên hsün," p. 3.

⑥   Not only do most Chinese myths have a long history and varied forms, but the texts in which they occur require critical examination.

older than the other sources quoted,[1] and therefore the original form of the myth can hardly be determined. Tradition is very persistent, and the later, cruder versions may really be earlier in their origin. But on the other hand, where such stories first appear in the late Chou and Han literature, it is often impossible to tell whether they were a part of the old Chinese culture, or represent external influence. The fact that a legend is crude is not necessarily a sign that it is old.

In the instance of this sun myth, we can be fairly sure that we are dealing with a myth of Northern China, where the characteristically Chinese culture arose, because in the *Li sao* of Ch'ü Yüan there is found a different sun myth which represents southern tradition.[2] In this legend the god of the sun is Tung Chün. The passage runs as follows: "The morning sun, rising from the east, shone through Fu sang. The sparkling night dawned gradually as he drove along in his dragon chariot through the thunder. The insignia and flags of cloud floated, and he sighed, hesitated, and looked back. He was clad with a coat of blue cloud and apron of white rainbow. He raised his long arrows and shot the heavenly wolves. After killing them he marched victoriously westward and sank to the depth of darkness, only to rise again

---

① The date of the compilation of the *Shu ching* is a disputed question which we cannot discuss here.

② The *Li sao* is a great repository of myths of Southern China, the modern provinces of Hupei and Hunan. At the time it was written, the third century B.C., there was sharp contrast in the mode of thinking and in literature between the North and the South. Here *Li sao* is used as a general title for all the works of Ch'ü Yüan as collected in the *Ch'u tz'ü* (楚辞).

in the east next morning." [①] The long arrows are symbolical of the sun's rays, and the heavenly wolves, of evil and darkness. It is a mistake for Ferguson to group this southern sun god with historical personages like Chang Liang and Kuan Yü, as he does in chapter eight.

Occult practices sometimes find their authorization in myths, and Dr. Ferguson devotes a chapter to the occult, but while he tells stories about divination, alchemy, geomancy, and other interesting subjects, he does not mention any myths in connection with them. And he writes (p. 137) as if he were not sure whether the "transmutation system" and the *Book of Changes* were two things or one. As a matter of fact, the "transmutation system" is the *Book of Changes*, and Wên Wang was not the sole author, but only one of those to whom the book is attributed.

Chinese folklore is very rich, and Dr. Ferguson devotes a chapter to it. It is, moreover, a question much discussed in scholarly circles in China at present. Yet such important tales as the *Mêng chiang nü,* [②] the *Liang shan po* and the *Chu ying-t'ai* are not mentioned. Instead, Dr. Ferguson has resorted to works of pure fiction shaped for literary purposes.[③] It would be interesting to know where Dr. Ferguson got his statement that Chung Kuei (p. 152) was

---

[①]   *Ch'u tz'ü*, "Chiu ko," Tung Chün. Not an exact translation, but adapted and abridged.

[②]   One of the most widely distributed of the Chinese folk-tales. Ku Chieh-kang, the author of the *Ku shih p'ien* has done much work on it.

[③]   *Liao chai ckih i* (Strange stories from a Chinese studio), p. 156. *Chin ku Ch'i kuan* (Curious stories of the past and present), p. 169. *Tung chou lieh kuo chih* (Records of the Eastern Chou dynasty: a historical novel), p. 166.

a scholar of the Sung period. [1] In the story of the "White Serpent" (pp. 158 160) the most important part, dealing with her love affair, the "Thunder Peak Pagoda" under which the serpent spirit is supposed to be imprisoned, and with the "Monastery of the Golden Mountain," the connection with the "Dragon Boat Festival" and with the Buddhist monk Fa Hai, is entirely omitted.

In the chapter on "Buddhistic Myths" Dr. Ferguson has mistaken the *Hsi yu chi* of Li Chih ch'ang for another book of the same title by Wu Ch'êng ên. He says: "One of the most noted mythological accounts is that of the adventures of Yüan Chuang, a priest of the Seventh century, who travelled to India in search of Buddhist books. On his return he dictated an account of his travels to Pien Chi, and his narrative is chiefly concerned with a description of the various countries through which he had passed during his journey of sixteen years. This book is called *Ta T'ang Hsi Yu Chi* ('Western travels in the T'ang Dynasty ').[2] During the Yüan dynasty the noted Taoist Ch'iu Ch'u chi was sent by the Emperor Genghis khan to India and was accompanied by his pupil Li Chih ch'ang. On their return Li wrote the account of their wanderings and of the miraculous events which he had learned to have happened to the priest Yüan Chuang on his earlier visit. The

---

[1]　For an authoritative account see, Chao I, *Kai yü ts'ung k'ao*, bk. 35.

[2]　A correct translation would be: "A T'ang record of Western Regions."

title of Li's book is taken from the earlier one, and it is called *Hsi Yu Chi*.①
This later book is full of miraculous events, which, although they are
interpreted from a Taoist standpoint, are all connected with the Buddhistic
monk Yüan Chuang, and for this reason are classified under the heading of
Buddhistic myths. The first part of this book contains an account of the
wonderful genealogy of Yüan Chuang."

Li Chih-ch'ang's *Hsi yu chi* is a book of travel recording the journey
of Ch'iu Ch'u-chi to the camps of Yüan T'ai-Tsu. Ch'iu Ch'u-chi was the
most famous Taoist of his time, and his Taoist title was Ch'ang Ch'un Tzŭ.
So the full title of this little book is called *Ch'ang Ch'un chên jen hsi yu
chi*.② As the facts recorded in it are mostly authentic, it is considered a very
important book on early geography and travels, and it tells absolutely
nothing of the travels of the Buddhistic monk Yüan Chuang and his
genealogy. It also had no connection with the *Ta T'ang hsi yü chi*, which
records the travels of Yüan Chuang. Dr. Ferguson apparently mistook Li
Chih ch'ang's *Hsi yu chi* for Wu Ch'êng-ên's *Hsi yu chi* because "the
wonderful genealogy of Yüan Chuang" which he gives in the next four

---

① It literally means "Record of Western Wanderings." *Ta T'ang hsi yü chi* and *Hsi yu chi*, although they sound nearly the same when romanized, are quite different in meaning. To regard the latter as a derivation from the former is entirely unwarranted.

② The work has been translated by Arthur Waley into English under the title of *The Travels of an Alchemist, the journey of the Taoist Ch'an-Ch'un from China to the Hindu Kush at the summons of Gingiz Khan, recorded by his disciple Li Chih-ch'ang*. Bretschneider's translation, Waley says, is an inaccurate abridgement of the Russian translation by Palladius.

pages of his book (pp. 190-193), was abridged from the ninth chapter of Wu Ch'êng-ên's book. Li's book and Wu's have no connection with each other except a similarity of titles.

These points are enough to show the defects of Dr. Ferguson's work. Other errors might be mentioned, such as his mistaking the tortoise for the turtle [1] as the worst kind of vilification, and the misconception of its origin from the green turban outcast class which he wrongly attributed to the T'ang dynasty.[2] Other anachronisms occur as on p. 20, "From the time of Chang to that of T'ai Tsung at the opening of the *Han dynasty*, the influence of the conservative School and the Confucian classics was at a low ebb...," and again on pp. 140-1, "The development of the science into the determination of the fortunes of relatives and descendants according to the lucky or

---

[1] Pointed out by Sowerby in his review in the *China Journal*, Dec.,1928, pp. 285–286 .

[2] "No worse term of abuse can be employed than to call another man a tortoise. The generally accepted explanation of this use of the term is that the outcast class (*lo hu*) who had no legal status, was obliged during the T'ang dynasty to wear a strip of green cloth tied around the head. The degenerate males of this outcast class lived from the earnings of the prostitution of their wives and daughters. This was the very lowest depth of immorality. As the head of the tortoise is green it became a symbol of the green beaded outcast; and to call a person a tortoise originally meant to put him in the vilest class of human beings, and also to name him as bastard," pp. 101.

This is guess work without any historical foundation. The tabu on the turtle did not begin in the T'ang dynasty. We can quote many illustrious names of the T'ang and Sung, and even the Yüan dynasties, named after the term *kuei*. It is only after the Yüan dynasty that such personal names became rare, and at present even words of the same sound are avoided in naming a person. So Chao I in his *Kai yü ts'ang k'ao* (bk. 38, pp. 23-24) says that the tabu began in the Yüan dynasty and became prevalent in the Ming period. Although the wearing of a green turban as a sign of disgrace can be traced back as early as the sixth century B.C., it was not officially instituted until the fourteenth century A.D. in the Ming dynasty. (See Lang Ying, *Ch'i hsiu lei kao*, bk. 28, pp. ll, 1880 Canton edition; and Chao I, *Kai yü ts'ung k'ao*, bk. 38, p. 25). "That the outcast class (*lo hu*)... was obliged in the T'ang dynasty to wear a strip of green cloth tied around the head" is without historical foundation. The use of the term "turtle" in vilification, so far as present evidence goes, has no actual connection with Dr. Ferguson's green turbaned outcast class.

unlucky site of the grave of a deceased person, was a development later than the time of *Kuo P'o* in the Han dynasty...".[1]

It is not the purpose of this paper to evaluate Dr. Ferguson's book, but only to point out its mistakes and deficiencies. It must be evident that they are serious enough to make the task necessary. A large part of the work does not deal with mythology proper at all. It is as if one were to write on English mythology by giving accounts of Berkeley and Hume, "Mother Goose," "Macbeth," "The Idyls of the King," selections from Lord Dunsany and Bram Stoker, and the *Book of Common Prayer*, with a few pictures of cathedrals and of such celebrities as Guy Fawkes thrown in for local color. Where myths are mentioned, they are not critically dealt with, and there are many misstatements of fact.

No scientific treatment of Chinese mythology exists in English. Probably the task is an impossible one for any westerner at present. Yet it is important for western scholars in other fields to realize that this is the case, and that this work of Dr. Ferguson cannot be considered as adequate or reliable.[2]

[与 J. K. Shryock 合作，原载 *Journal of the American Oriental Society* Vol.53(1933),pp.53−65]

---

[1]　Kuo P'o was born in 276 A.D.,more than half a century later than the last of the Hans.

[2]　There are many myths which Dr. Fergnson has not considered,such as the Chinese flood myth and the occupational myths. The Chinese flood myth represents a different aspect of this widely distributed story. The other flood myths usually say that God sent the flood to destroy men on account of their wickedness, or merely as a general inundation, but the Chinese myth embodies the idea of controlling the water and the formation of the water-ways by human or supernatural agencies.

THE BLACK MAGIC IN CHINA
KNOWN AS *KU*①

A number of ideas and practices are grouped together under the Chinese term *ku*.② These ideas and practices justify the use of the phrase "Black Magic"; that is, magic whose purpose is to injure someone. In this sense the word is contrasted with *wu*,③ "White Magic," or magic whose purpose is beneficial. The phrase "Black Magic" is too general, however, for the Chinese term *ku* refers to certain particular methods of black magic, which are, so far as the authors are aware, peculiar to certain cultures of Southeastern

---

①　The preparation of this article was made possible by a grant from the Faculty Research Fund of the University of Pennsylvania.

②　蠱; formed by Ch'ung (insects, worms, etc.) 虫 over min (vessel, dish) 皿.

③　巫.

Asia. In ancient times this specific feature of culture may have been spread over a wider area.

At present, *ku* is used primarily as a means of acquiring wealth; secondarily as a means of revenge. The method is to place poisonous snakes and insects together in a vessel until there is but one survivor, which is called the *ku*. The poison secured from this *ku* is administered to the victim, who becomes sick and dies. The ideas associated with *ku* vary, but the *ku* is generally regarded as a spirit, which secures the wealth of the victim for the sorcerer.

Archaeological evidence indicates that the word *ku* is at least as ancient as the Chinese script itself. The earliest reliable specimens of Chinese writing are inscriptions on the shells of tortoises and on the shoulder blades of cattle, found in a Yin Shang site at An-yang, Honan, in 1899. An ancient form of the word *ku* has been identified on these fragments. This form is more pictorial than the present form of the word, and shows clearly two insects in a receptacle.[1]

This written word therefore has existed in approximately its present form for at least three thousand years. The ideographic nature of Chinese writing and the continuity of Chinese literature have the effect that while a written symbol may acquire new meanings and associations in the course of time, these seldom entirely supersede and eliminate the older meanings, as

---

[1]　殷墟文字类编 chüan 13. By 罗振玉，商承祚编.

may happen in phonetic systems. Consequently, while some of the meanings attached to the word *ku* may be older than others, we can be fairly sure that the oldest meaning has not been lost.

The *Shuo wen*, a dictionary of about A.D. 100, says, "*Ku* is worms in the belly. The commentary on the *Spring and Autumn Annals* (the *Tso chuan*) says, 'Vessel and worms make *ku*, caused by licentiousness. Those who have died violent deaths are also *ku*.'① The word vessel signifies the utility of the thing." As is indicated by this definition, the Chinese written word is formed by the radical meaning "insects" or "worms" placed above the radical meaning "vessel" or "dish."

In the Pre-Han literature, the word is used in five different ways. It indicates (1) a disease, (2) evil spirits, (3) to cause doubt, or a woman inveigling a man, (4) a worm-eaten vessel, and grain which moulders and is blown away, and (5) a divination symbol. Some of these meanings have become attached to the word by analogy.

The use of *ku* as a disease may be illustrated by a passage from the *Tso chuan*.

"In the first year of Duke Chao (541 B.C.), the marquis of Chin asked the help of a physician from Ch'in, and the earl of Ch'in sent one named Ho to see him. Ho said, 'The disease cannot be cured. It is said that when women are approached [too frequently] the result is a disease resembling

---

① This passage is later quoted in full.

ku. It is not caused by a spirit, nor by food (the methods of magic); it is a delusion which has destroyed the mind.'" When asked what he meant by *ku*, he replied, "'I mean that 〔disease〕 which is produced by excessive sexual indulgence. Consider the word; it is formed by the words for vessel and for insects. It is also used for grain which 〔moulders and〕 flies away. In the *Book of Changes*, a woman deluding a man, and wind throwing down 〔the trees of〕 a mountain, are *ku*. All these have the same signification.'"

The fundamental idea of *ku* as a disease is based on an analogy. The human body is regarded as a vessel, into which the disease spirits enter like insects. Many early peoples have regarded disease as due to the possession of the body by an alien spirit. Excessive sexual indulgence causes a man to lose his virility, his soul. This is not *ku*, but the effect is similar to the effect of *ku*. Therefore a woman inveigling a man has come by analogy to be called *ku*.

It will be shown that ancient Chinese ideas associated the wind with the generation of worms. This is applied to mouldering grain, either in the sense that the chaff is blown away by the wind, or that worms generate in the grain, become insects and fly away. It appears that the essential idea behind these meanings of *ku* is a loss of soul.

In the *Shih chi feng ch'an shu*,[1] it is said that "Duke Teh of Chin instituted the *fou* sacrifice, killing dogs at the four gates of the city to dispel

---

[1]　史记封禅书.

the *ku* plague." The *Ch'in pen chi*[1] says, "In the second year (of Duke Tek) dogs were killed to ward off *ku*." Dogs have frequently been used in Chinese apotropaic practices, from ancient times until the present.

In the *Shan hai ching* [2]it is said, "Again east 300 li, there is the mountain called Ching chiu, and there is an animal like the fox, having nine tails and the voice of a baby. It eats men, but those who eat it are immune to *ku*." A commentary remarks on this passage,[3] that such men will not "encounter evil atmosphere." This appears to identify *ku* with malignant atmospheric conditions, something like poison gas. But it might also be interpreted as indicating the presence of evil spirits, or something created by black magic.

Cheng Ssu nung, in his commentary on the *Ta tsung po*,[4] said, "At present, people kill dogs in sacrifice to stop the wind." Kuo P'u ,[5] in his commentary on the *Erh ya*, remarks, "The modern custom of sacrificing dogs in the highways is said to stop the wind." Such customs are very old, and have survived to the present in the belief that the blood of black dogs is an effective antidote to magic. While these latter references are not from pre- Han literature, they probably reflect pre-Han beliefs.

---

[1] Chap. 5 of the *Shih chi*. The passage is quoted by De Groot, *Religious System of China*, Vol. V, p. 826.

[2] 山海经第一南山经.

[3] Ibid.,Commentary by Kuo P'u 郭璞.

[4] 周礼注疏 chüan 18 , 春官大宗伯引郑司农注.

[5] 尔雅·释天第八 "祭风曰磔" commentary by Kuo P'u.

The *Book of Changes* is an ancient work on divination, consisting of the explanations of sixty-four hexagrams, or figures secured in divination. The eighteenth hexagram is formed by the *ken* trigram placed above the *sun* trigram. The *ken* trigram is a symbol of mountains, of resting and stopping, and of the youngest son. The *sun* trigram symbolizes wind or wood, flexibility, penetration, and oldest daughter. The entire hexagram is called *ku*. The text of the *Book of Changes* dealing with the hexagram as a whole, which is probably the oldest strata of the text, is as follows:

"*Ku* indicates great progress and success. There will be advantage in crossing the great river."... This means that when a man divined, and secured the hexagram *ku*, the omen was auspicious. It meant that the one who divined would be successful, while his enemies would be injured. Crossing the river was equivalent to an offensive military expedition. The way in which the hexagram *ku* was used in practice may be illustrated by an incident from the *Tso chuan*.

"In the eleventh month of the fifteenth year of Duke He, the marquis of Chin and the earl of Ch'in fought at Han, and the marquis of Chin was taken. Before the expedition, the earl of Ch'in asked his diviner, T'u-fu, to consult the milfoil, and he replied,"

"'A lucky response; if they cross the river, the chariots of the marquis will be defeated.'"

"The earl asked to have the matter more fully explained."

"The diviner said, 'It is very lucky. You will defeat his troops three times, and finally capture the marquis of Chin. The figure found is *ku*', of which it is said,"

"The thousand chariots are put to flight three times."

"Then you catch what remains, called the fox."

"That fox in *ku* must be the marquis of Chin. Moreover, the inner symbol of *ku* represents wind, while the outer represents mountains. It is now autumn. We gather the fruit on the hills, and we shake the trees; it is plain we are to be victorious. The fruit falls down, and the trees are all shaken; what can this be but the defeat of Chin ? "

The present text of the *Book of Changes* cannot be older than the Chou period, but the hexagrams are much older. Chinese tradition says that there were different explanations given to the hexagrams in the Hsia and Shang periods. The oracle bones show that the word *ku*, written as insects in a vessel, was in existence during the Shang period. The authors of this monograph advance the theory that if we had the Shang explanations of the hexagrams, the two trigrams which in the Chou period were held to represent mountains and wind, would be found to represent vessel and insects.

In using eight symbols to represent many things, each symbol must do more than single duty. The written Chinese words for mountains and vessel are very similar. The theory advanced is that the trigram which in the Chou period symbolized mountains, in the Shang period symbolized vessel. This is merely an hypothesis.

But in the case of the other trigram there is very good evidence for the association of insects and wind, *Huai-nan Tzu* says:[1]

"Heaven is one. Earth is two. Man is three. Three times three is nine. Two times nine is eighteen. The number eight stands for wind. Wind represents worms. Therefore worms are transformed in eight days." It will be noticed that the number eighteen is the number of the hexagram *ku*.

The *Shuo wen*, in defining the character feng (wind), says, "When the wind blows, worms generate. Therefore worms are transformed in eight days."

A commentator on this passage, Hsü Hao,[2] says, "The wind has no form that can be pictured, so the character is made from the thing which the wind generates. Therefore the radical 'worm' is the base of the character 'wind.' When the geomancer is searching for a favorable spot in the country, he observes where the wind goes, and he knows that below that spot there are ants. This is the verification of the expression, 'The wind blows, and worms generate.'"

Although the *Huai-nan Tzu* and the *Shuo wen* belong to the Han period, the belief in the connection between the wind and worms must be very old, since the character for wind is written with the radical for worms. The

---

① 淮南子, 坠形训.
② 说文徐笺.

connection appears to have been forgotten, since the *Tso chuan* interprets the hexagram as wind blowing down mountains, an interpretation which does not make sense. The hypothesis advanced here, which does not seem to have occurred to scholars, is that the original meaning of the hexagram was not mountains and wind, but worms in a vessel. This idea is clearly indicated by the written form of *ku* on the oracle bones. And as *ku* was a kind of black magic, the hypothesis explains why the hexagram indicated success to the diviner and injury to his opponent. That was the purpose of black magic.[①]

The *Chou li* says, describing a part of the ancient administration,[②] "The department consisted of an official and four assistants. They were in charge of the extermination of the poisonous *ku*. They drove it out by spells, and attacked it by efficacious herbs. They directed those who could control

---

[①] European scholars have done little work on the subject of *ku*. It is mentioned by Granet, *Chinese Civilization*, p. 254, and by A. Conrady, "Yih-King-Studien," *Asia Major*, Vol. VII, 1932, p. 418, who translates the term as "Hexenkessel." The practice of *ku* among the Miao is mentioned by S. R. Clarke, *Among the Tribes of South-west China*, China Inland Mission, 1911, pp. 70, 71. E. T. Williams, "Witchcraft in the Chinese Penal Code," *Jour. North China Branch, Royal Asiatic Society*, Vol. XXXVIII, 1907, pp. 61-96, gives a brief description of *ku*, and of legal efforts to stamp it out. The fullest treatment of *ku* in a European work is in J. J. M. De Groot, *Religious System of China*, Vol. V, pp. 826-69. De Groot devotes a chapter to the subject. But unfortunately half his space is filled with a description of the *Wu-ku* Rebellion under Han Wu Ti. *Wu-ku* was a general term ("White and Black Magic") for any sort of magic, and the rebellion, as well as the conspiracy under the Empress Teng 200 years later, had nothing to do with the peculiar methods of *ku*. De Groot's treatment is unsatisfactory in other respects.

[②] No attempt is made here to give the various legal enactments against the practice of *ku*. The penal code of the T'ang dynasty on this subject has generally continued in force, and is quoted in later dynastic codes. The practice of *ku* is called an inhuman crime. One who makes *ku*, or instructs in its use, is hanged, his property confiscated, his family and the inmates of his house are banished 3,000 li, etc. 唐律疏议 chüan 18.

ku, and watched the effect." ①

Cheng K'ang-ch'eng's commentary on this passage in the *Chou li* quotes the criminal law of the Han dynasty as saying, "Those who dare to poison people with *ku*, or teach others to do it, will be publicly executed." The law of the Han was based on earlier codes, going back at least to the fourth century B.C., and it is not unlikely that the practice of *ku* was forbidden from the time of the first legal codes in China, perhaps long before. If *ku* always represented a method of injuring others, this is what we would expect, since black magic is usually illegal.

In Ku Yeh wang's *Yü ti chih*② it is said, "In several provinces south of the Yangtse river, there are people who keep *ku*. The host uses it to kill people. He puts it in food or drink, and the victims do not realize its presence. If the family of the keeper of the *ku* all die, the *ku* flies about without any objective. Any one who encounters it is killed." The *Yü ti chih* is a work of the sixth century A.D., the period of the Six Dynasties, corresponding to the early middle ages in Europe.

In the *Sou shen chi*③ of Kan Pao,④ attributed to the fourth century A.D., is the following passage:

---

① Chap. 37. De Groot quotes this passage, p. 826, but mistranslates the last phrase.

② 與地志. By 顾野王, A.D. 519 81. A scholar and official.

③ 搜神记 chüan 12.

④ 干宝. 4th Cent. A.D. The author flourished under Chin Yüan Ti. His book is a collection of supernatural tales. De Groot quotes these stories (p. 846), but misreads the author's surname as Yü. Giles, *Biog. Dict.*, p. 357, uses the correct form.

"In the province of Yung-yang, there was a family by the name of Liao. For several generations they manufactured *ku*, becoming rich from it. Later one of the family married, but they kept the secret from the bride. On one occasion, everyone went out except the bride, who was left in charge of the house. Suddenly she noticed a large cauldron in the house, and on opening it, perceived a big snake inside. She poured boiling water into the cauldron and killed the snake. When the rest of the family returned she told them what she had done, to their great alarm. Not long after, the entire family died of the plague." Kan Pao also mentions a variety called "dog *ku*" and says that the magic can take the forms of various animals.

"Chao Shou of the P'o-yang district possessed dog *ku*. Once a man named Ch'en Tsen visited Chao, when he was attacked by six or seven large yellow dogs. Yu Hsiang-po[①] (another man) once ate with Chao's wife. Later he almost died from hemorrhage, and was saved by drinking a medicine prepared from the roots of the orange tree. *Ku* has a strange, ghostly appearance. It can appear in many forms, as dogs, pigs, worms or snakes. It is not recognized by the man himself. All who get it, die."

In the *Sou shen hou chi*:[②] "Tan Yu was a poor and devout monk. There was a family in the district of Yen who manufactured *ku*. Those who ate their food died from hemorrhage. Tan Yu once visited this family, and the

---

① De Groot translates Yu Hsiang po as "paternal uncle," but *hsiang* is not a relationship term.

② 搜神后记, chüan 2. Attributed to T'ao Chien 陶潜, a famous poet.

host prepared food for him. Tan Yu recited an incantation, and saw a pair of centipedes a foot, long suddenly crawl away from the dish. He then ate the food, and returned home without being harmed."

In the biography of Ku Chi chih in the Liu Sung history (A.D. 420 479), an instance of *ku* poisoning is recorded. "T'ang Tzu, of the Hsiang district, went to Chu Ch'i's mother P'en's house to drink wine. On returning home he became ill, and vomitted more than ten *ku* worms. Seeing that he was about to die, he directed his wife Chang that after death she should cut open his abdomen in order to get rid of the disease. Later Chang cut open his body, and saw his 'five viscera' completely destroyed." [1]

These instances from the medieval period of Chinese history indicate a view that *ku* was a kind of poison which was administered in food and drink. A little later a medical work, the *Tsao shih chu ping yüan hou tsung lun* [2] of the Sui period (A.D. 589-618) describes how this poison was manufactured.

"There are several kinds of *ku*. All of them are poisonous. People sometimes deliberately prepare *ku*. They take worms, insects, snakes, and other poisonous creatures, and put them together in a vessel. They allow them to eat each other until only one is left, and this survivor is the *ku*. The *ku* can change its appearance and bewitch people. When put in food and

---

[1]　The narrative goes on to say that the widow was accused of the crime of mistreating her husband's corpse. The case was brought before Ku Chi-chih, who acquired considerable reputation from the way he handled it.

[2]　巢氏诸病源候总论, chüan 25. A medical work of the Sui period.

drink, it causes disease and calamity (to the one who eats it). There is also 'flying *ku*'. It comes and goes without one's knowledge, and eventually appears somewhat like a ghost. Those who have seen it, die."

This appears to be the earliest account, not later than A.D. 600, of how this magical process was carried out. It gives a reasonable explanation of the formation of the written word, formed of insects and dish. The explanation is still more suitable for the pictograph found on the oracle bones of the Shang period.

The idea behind this practice is quite reasonable. If centipedes and snakes are poisonous individually, the survivor of such a group, who has eaten the others, is considered to combine with himself the collected venom of the group. If a man desires to injure an enemy, no more formidable weapon could be put into his hand. The difficulty is to say when this rational, if mistaken, process becomes pure magic. Action at a distance does not seem to be one of the properties of *ku*. Poisoning and magic are found together in all countries, from the days of Medea. Some of the stories are pure magic, while others indicate no more than a use of poison.

The evidence presented so far may be summarized. The word itself goes back to the oldest written records of the Chinese language. The pictograph clearly shows insects, worms, or snakes in a receptable. But in the ancient literature of the Chou period, the word is used in a number of ways, of which the most important and primary appear to be as a diseased condition and as a divination symbol. How far may a magical practice first described clearly about A.D. 600 be ascribed to the period before 500 B.C.?

The literature which has survived from the Chou period has been carefully edited, for the most part by Confucians, beginning, according to tradition, with Confucius himself. In their desire to idealize the past, and to show, not what really occurred, but what ought to have occurred, they have created great difficulties for the ethnologist.

But it often happens that ideas and practices which are never mentioned in literature, especially in moral, religious, and philosophic literature, survive unchanged in the lives of the people. The explanation that *ku* was originally a magical practice agrees with the pictograph on the oracle bones, with the use of the word to describe a disease, and with its use in divination. The *Tso chuan* indicates that in divination, the symbol indicated that the diviner would be successful in injuring his enemy. In the Han period, the term was used for black magic, and in the medieval period, for a magical method of poisoning an enemy. Therefore it seems reasonable to assume that the term always stood for black magic.

Early Chinese literature describes the culture of the valley of the Yellow River. Later literature indicates that the practice of *ku* extended at one time over the whole area included in China proper. This was probably true long before there is any evidence from the Yangtse valley, or the more southern regions. Even in the medieval period, Chinese observers remarked on the prevalence of the practice in southern China, and from the T'ang period on, the practice appears to have been more and more confined to aboriginal tribes of the south. The policy of repression definitely stated by Cheng K'ang-ch'eng in his commentary on the *Chou li* appears to have been largely effective throughout the more characteristically Chinese areas, and later writers notice the practice of *ku* in the south as a peculiar phenomenon. Nevertheless, the practice of *ku* seems to have been a specific cultural feature which the ancient inhabitants of the Yellow River valley shared with the inhabitants of more southern areas.

The *Ling piao lu i* [1] of Liu Shun, written about A.D. 900, which is one of the earliest geographic works dealing with Kuangtung and the adjacent southern areas, contains the following passage:

"The mountains and rivers of Ling-piao wind and cluster together. It is not easy to go out or come in. Therefore the district abounds in fogs and mists which become pestilential vapors. People exposed to them are liable to become sick. Their stomachs swell, and they become *ku*. It is popularly said that there are persons who collect poisonous insects in order to make *ku* and poison people. I think that this is due to the humidity of the place, which causes poisonous creatures to flourish there, and not because the people of Ling-piao are cruel by nature."

---

[1]　岭表录异, chüan 1. A work of the T'ang period, and one of the earliest geographical works now existing about Kuangtung and the adjacent areas.

From the Sung period on (beginning about A.D. 960), all references to *ku* assign its practice to the tribes of the southwest. There is an instance recorded in the *Ling wai tai ta* of Chou ch'u-fei [①].

"The *ku* poison of Kuangsi is of two kinds. One kind kills a man quickly, while the other works gradually and does not kill for six months. If a man has a grudge against anyone, he is courteous to him, but poisons him secretly. After half a year, the poison takes effect. The murderer cannot be brought to law, and the poisoning cannot be cured. This is the most cruel form of *ku*. In 1170, on the eastern side of Ching-chou, there was a seller of sauce who prepared *ku*. It was discovered, and the man executed. It is said that when his family prepared *ku*, the women, naked and with dishevelled hair, made a nightly sacrifice of a dish of deermeat soup. Grasshoppers, butterflies, and all kinds of insects came down from the roof and ate the soup. That which they emitted was the poison. If anyone wishes to know whether a family keeps *ku* poison, they call tell from the cleanliness of the house. If everything is kept very clean, then the family has *ku*. When the natives of Li-T'ung and Chi-T'ung (in southwestern China) invite guests to a feast, the host must first taste the food in order to convince the guests that there are no grounds for suspicion."

There is a somewhat similar reference in the gazetteer of Yung-fu, a

---

① 岭外代答,chüan 10. By 周去非 . The author was assistant sub-prefect of Kuei-lin, in Kuangsi, during the years A.D. 1174-89. The story is given by De Groot, p. 848.

district of Kuangsi.[1] *Ku* poison is not found generally among the people (i.e. the Chinese), but is used by the T'ung[2] women. It is said that on the fifth day of the fifth month,[3] they go to a mountain stream and spread new clothes and headgear on the ground, with a bowl of water beside them. The women dance and sing naked, inviting a visit from the King of Medecine (a tutelary spirit). They wait until snakes, lizards, and poisonous insects come to bathe in the bowl. They pour the water out in a shadowy, damp place. Then they gather the fungus (poisonous?) which grows there, which they mash into a paste. They put this into goose-feather tubes, and hide them in their hair. The heat of their bodies causes worms to generate, which resemble newly-hatched silk-worms. Thus *ku* is produced. It is often concealed in a warm, damp place in the kitchen.

"The newly made *ku* is not yet poisonous. It is used as a love potion, administered in food and drink, and called 'love-medicine.'[4] Gradually the *ku* becomes poisonous. As the poison develops, the woman's body itches until she has poisoned someone. If there is no other opportunity, she will poison even her husband or her sons, but she possesses antidotes."

"It is believed that those who produce *ku* themselves become *ku* after

---

① 永福县志; quoted by Wang Sen 汪森, in his 粤西丛载, chüan18.

② "獞". The chief aboriginal tribe of Kuangsi.

③ The fifth day of the fifth month is an important day in the Chinese religious calendar, the day of the "Dragon Boat Festival." The story told in connection with it dates from the 3rd Cent. B.C., but the festival is probably much older.

④ 和合药 or 粘食药.

death. The ghosts of those who have died from the poison become their servants. So a majority of the foolish T'ung make this thing. When a man enters a house in a T'ung village, if he sees no ashes on the hearth, and if the faces of the women appear yellow and their eyes red, he knows that there is *Ku* in that house. Bronze chop sticks are used as a charm against *ku*. Dipped into poisoned food, they cause it to turn black..."

A similar case is recorded in the *Shuang huai sui ch'ao.* [①] "During the reign of Cheng T'ung (1436-49), Chon Li of the district of Wu-chiang traded in Ssu-eng of Kuangsi, and married a widowed daughter of the Cheng family. He remained there twenty years, until their son was sixteen. One day Chou Li wanted to return home. His wife was unable to dissuade him, but she put *ku* in Chou Li's food without his knowledge. She bade her son follow him, and told the boy secretly that if his father promised to come back, he should cure him. For this purpose she taught him the antidote. When Chou Li reached home the *ku* began to affect him. His belly became swollen, and he drank water excessively. His son asked the date on which he would return to his wife.

"Chou Li replied, 'I also think of your mother, but I am sick. How can I go back ? As soon as I get a little better, I shall start.'"

"The son replied, 'I can cure the disease.' He bound his father to a

---

① 双槐岁抄,chüan 5. By 黄瑜. 15th Cent. A.D. Chronological records of miscellaneous facts from 1368 (the beginning of the Ming dynasty) to 1487.

pillar. Chou Li was thirsty and asked for a drink. His son offered him a clay bowl filled with water, but when it was almost at his mouth, the boy threw it away. This happened several hundred times. Chou Li became so thirsty that he could hardly bear it. Shortly after, he vomited out a small carp, which was still alive. The swelling soon disappeared, and he was cured. Among the barbarians there are many *ku* poisons so made as to become effective at a certain date. After that date, the case cannot be cured. Widows are called 'ghosts' wives, and men dare not approach them. When strangers marry them, they are usually poisoned."

There is a reference to *ku* in the *shu i chi*[1]. "In Tien (Yun-nan) there are many *ku* sorcerers, especially among the women. They often seduce men. If the beloved was about to go on a long journey, he was always poisoned with *ku*. If the man did not return on the promised date, he died. There was a traveler who went to Tien and loved a woman. When he was leaving the place, the woman said to him, 'I have already poisoned you with *ku*. If you do not return as you have promised, your belly will swell, and then you must come to me as quickly as possible. After a month, it will be incurable.' On that day the man's belly really became swollen. He hesitated to return; then his abdomen burst, and he died. People found in his belly a wooden trough for feeding pigs. It is certainly strange !"

---

[1] 述异记, chüan 2. By 东轩主人 (a pen name). The author is unknown. The facts recorded occurred under the Manchu reigns Shun-chih and K'ang-hsi, about the middle of the 17th Cent. It treats of the supernatural, and was published in 1701.

It is significant that in these stories all the practitioners of this love magic are women of the aboriginal tribes of the southwest.

In the *Sui shu ti li chih*① it is recorded that "the inhabitants of these districts (in Kiangsi and some other areas south of the Yangtse) often kept *ku* poison, and the practice was especially prevalent in I-Ch'un. The method is, on the fifth day of the fifth month to collect all kinds of insects and worms, from snakes to lice, putting them together in a vessel, where they devour each other. The survivor is kept. If it should be a snake, it is snake-*ku*. If a louse, then it is louse-*ku*. This *ku* is used to kill people. It is administered through food, and afterwards it consumes the victim's internal organs. When the person dies, his property is moved by the *ku* spirit to the house of the keeper of the *ku*. If for three years the keeper does not kill a man with the *ku*, the keeper himself is killed by it. It is handed down from generation to generation, and is given to a daughter as a dowry. Kan Pao (the author of the *Sou shen chi*) regarded *ku* as a spirit, but this view is mistaken. During the rebellion of Hou Ching, most of the *ku*-keeping families perished. Since the *ku* had no master, it wandered about the roads, and those who met it, died."

Another variety of *ku* is called the "golden caterpillar," or *chintsan*. Li

---

① 隋书·地理志, chüan 31. The geographical section of the Sui dynasty history.

Shih-chen in the *Pen tsao kang mu* [①] quotes Ch'en Tsang-chi of the T'ang period as follows: "The ashes of old satin can cure 'the *ku* worms which eat satin.' The commentary says, 'The *worm* crawls like a finger ring. It eats old satin brocade and other silk cloths, just as the silk-worm eats mulberry leaves.' In my opinion, this is the *chin-tsan*." According to Li, the golden caterpillars originated in Szechuan and from there made their way into the Hukuang provinces.

The *T'ieh wei shan tsung hua* of Tsai T'ao [②] says, "The *chintsa* poison began in Szechuan, but now it has spread to Hu, Kuang, Min and Yueh (Hupeh, Hunan, Kuangtung, Kuangsi, Fukien and Chekiang). There are people who give it away, and this is called 'giving the golden caterpillar a husband.' Those who do this place gold, ornaments for dressing the head, satin and brocade with the worm, and put it beside the road for others to find. The magistrate of Yü-lin told me that there was a legal case involving this practice in the district of Fu-Ch'ing. One man brought charge against another, stating that the latter had poisoned his family with *chin-tsan*. The magistrate could not find any evidence of such poison having been used. Then someone suggested bringing hedgehogs to the house of the accused.

---

① 本草纲目, chüan 42. By 李时珍. A well known medieal work containing extracts from more than 800 authors, and describing 1,892 medicines. The last half of the 16th Cent. De Groot makes considerable use of the work.

② 铁围山丛谈 chüan 6. By 蔡絛, First half of the 12th Cent. It treats of events contemporary with the author. The passage is quoted in part by De Groot, p. 850.

Since the *chin-tsan* is known to be afraid of hedgehogs, this advice was followed. The *chin-tsan* dared not move, although it hid in a hole under the bed. It was caught and pulled out by the two hedgehogs. It is really astonishing."[1]

The *Kua i chih*[2] says, "The *chin-tsan* is a caterpillar the color of gold. It is fed with Shu satin, and its excretions collected, which are then put into food and drink in order to poison people. Those who take it, die. Then the spirit of the worm is glad, and moves the valuables of the deceased to the house of the practitioner, making him suddenly rich. But to get rid of the worm is difficult, because water, fire and swords cannot harm it. The only way is to put gold and silver into a basket with the *chin-tsan*, and then place the basket beside a road. Someone passing by may take it. This is called 'giving the *chin-tsan* a husband.'"

The *Fan T'ien lu t'an tsung*[3] says, "The antidote for those poisoned by the *chin-tsan* is food from the home of one who has kept the *ku*. But it must be given by the keeper of the *ku* personally, for if it is given by anyone

---

[1]　Williams, "Witchcraft in the Chinese Penal Code," p. 91, quotes the *Hsi yüan lu* 洗冤录, a guide to magistrates in their duties as coroners, as saying that a medicine including two centipedes, one alive, one roasted, was a cure for *ku*. De Groot, pp. 863-69, gives a large number of remedies and antidotes for *ku*, collected from various medical works. They include musk, cinnabar, striped sats, dried centipedes (for snake-*ku*), leek-juice, and "thunder stones." These last are prehistoric implements, stone knives and axes, often found in Kuangtung and the island of Hainan. Domestic fowls are said to detect *ku*.

[2]　括异志. Quoted by De Groot, p. 854. By 鲁应龙 of the Sung period. Not to be confused with another book by the same name by 张师正.

[3]　梵天庐谈丛, chüan 33. By 柴萼. A work of miscellaneous notes, published by the Chung-hua Book Co. of Shanghai in 1926.

else, the antidote will not be effective. Hence if the person knows where he was poisoned, he can go to the man who poisoned him and beg him pitifully for relief. The man will not acknowledge the act at first, but after incessant pleading, he will angrily take a little food and throw it to the patient. On eating it, the victim will be cured instantly. When the appointed time for poisoning arrives and there are no outsiders present, even the keeper's own relatives may become his victims, for otherwise the spirit would cause a calamity of some sort. The spirit is appeased by the poisoning, because the spirits of the victims become his slaves."[1] There do not seem to be any descriptions of the way in which the *chin-tsan ku* is produced. It is said to be the third stage in the development of *ku*.

Another variety of *ku* poison is called *t'iao-sheng*,[2] This kind of *ku* is more clearly black magic. It is described in the *Ling wai tai ta*.[3] "In Kuangsi, those who kill people by *t'iao-sheng* bewitch the food, and invite guests to eat. When eaten, the fish and meat become alive again, living in the victim's stomach, and eventually kill him. It is currently believed that the spirits of those who have met death through *t'iao-sheng* become slaves in the home of the sorcerer. Once a celebrated scholar, while judge of Lei-chou (on the island of Hai-nan), had an experience with t'iao-sheng . He covered some meat with a plate and asked the culprit to bewitch it, in order to test the

---

[1] Ibid.

[2] 排生 . The phrase may be translated as "to revive," or "to become alive again."

[3] 岭外代答，chüan 10.

efficiency of his art. After a while he took up the plate, and hairs were growing out of the meat. What a devil it must be who can do this! Yet undoing the enchantment was quite easy. If you feel that the magic is in your stomach, take *sheng-ma* and vomit it out. Then if you feel the magic in your intestines, quickly take *yü-chin* and pass it out. This prescription was printed in Lei-chou for distribution and given to the people after it had been obtained from the culprit."

The *Ch'i hsiu lei kao*[1] says, "In Yunnan, Kueichou and Kuangsi, what is called *t'iao-sheng* is witchcraft. The sorcerer invites people to eat fish and meat which have been bewitched. When they have eaten them, the animals become alive again in their organs, and then proceed to kill the victims. I (the author) saw recorded in Fan Shih hu's *Kuei hai yü heng chih*[2] that there was at that time a man named Li Sou weng, a judge of Lei-chou. He secured a good prescription ... (then follows the prescription, which is similar to that in the preceding paragraph). Officials of the place are often attacked by this magic. The prescription is not readily available, so I publish it here."

The *Nan chung tsa chi*[3] says, "The chiefs of Yüan-chiang have handed down the method of producing *ku*. This medicine is not beneficent, but is poisonous. An astonishing fact is that when a new magistrate arrives the

---

[1]　七修类稿,chüan 45.事物类. By 郎英. A work of the Ming period.

[2]　桂海虞衡志. By 范成大.A work of the Sung period. It treated of the geography and natural history of the southern provinces.

[3]　南中杂记. By 刘崑. Miscellaneous facts about South China.

people must prepare a feast to welcome him, and they poison him then. The poison does not become effective during his term of office, but the pupils of his eyes turn from black to blue, and his face becomes pale and swollen. Then some months after he leaves office, his whole family die."

Again, in the same work: "The *ku* of the people of Burmah does not make use of medicine, but employs spirits. The spell is handed down from generation to generation. Within forty-nine days, they can bewitch a cow hide to the size of a mustard seed. They call this 'cow-hide *ku*.' They can also bewitch an iron ploughshare to the size of a mustard seed, and this they call 'ploughshare *ku*.' The method of applying such *ku* is to conceal the mustard seed under a finger-nail, and shoot it out toward the victim. The poison then enters his stomach. When a Chinese was affected by this poison, the Burmese would calculate the length of his journey, and chant the incantation. The *ku* poison would affect him on the calculated day. The victim would become thin, his abdomen would swell, and he would die within a few months. There was one man among the native chiefs called Yang Chao-pa, of the district of T'eng-yüeh, who could chant a counter spell which would cause the *ku* poison to leave the Chinese and attack the Burmese."

The *Po yüeh feng t'u chi* [1] says, "The *ku* drugs are not of one kind only, and the methods of using them differ. *Ku* sometimes changes the five

---

[1] 百越风土记.

viscera into earth or wood. Sometimes *ku* is put into chicken or duck meat. When the poison entered the stomach, the chicken or duck would become alive again, with wings and feet. It would compel the victim's soul to become a slave in the house of the sorcerer. When the Chinese caught such a sorcerer, they buried him alive, or burnt him."

The *Tien nan hsin yü* [1] says, "The Pa-yi (Shan) of the mountains (an aboriginal tribe in southwestern China) skin a cow and bewitch its hide to the size of a mustard seed. Those traders who entered the mountains without knowing this fact, sometimes had love affairs with the native girls. When they had sold their merchandise and were about to return home, the natives would invite them to a feast. At the feast, they would promise the girls to return. If they returned as they promised, they would be cured. But if they did not return, the *ku* poison (administered at the feast) became effective, and their bellies burst. The cow hides came out as if freshly skinned."

The *Ch'ih ya* [2] contains an interesting passage. "On the fifth day of the fifth month collect all those insects and worms that are poisonous, and put them together in a vessel. Let them devour each other, and the one finally remaining is called *ku*. There are snake *ku*, lizard *ku*, and dung-beetle *ku*. The length of time required for the insects to devour each other will be proportionate to the time required for the poisoned victim to die. When the *ku* has been

---

[1]　滇南新语. By 张泓. An account of Yunnan, written in the latter part of the 17th Cent.

[2]　赤雅. By 邝露, chüan 2. A description of the Miao country in Southwest China, written about the first part of the 17th Cent. The author was in the service of a native chieftaness for several years.

produced, the next step is to put it into food, which will then become a hundred times more delicious. Those who eat this food will die within a few days, or after a year of violent pains in the heart and stomach. The victim's property will imperceptibly be removed to the house of the witch, and his spirit becomes her slave, like the tiger which enslaves its *Ch'ang*. Later the *ku* flies about by night, appearing like a meteor. This variety is called 'flitting *ku*'. When the light grows stronger, a shadow like a living man's is produced. This is then called *t'iao-sheng ku*. When its shadow grows stronger, the *ku* can have intercourse with women. Then it is called *chin tsan ku*. It can go wherever it desires, and spreads calamity throughout the country-side. The more men it poisons, the more efficient the *ku* becomes, and the richer grows the witch. Among the aborigines, such evils are practiced openly. The native officials called Ti-to became aware of this, and asked a magician to dispel the enchantment. They caught the witch, and buried her alive with her head above the ground. They poured wax on her head and lighted it, in order to call back the poisoned spirits. The ghosts did not dare to approach, and the T'ung women cursed the witch for them. This is the only way to put a witch to death, for otherwise it is impossible to bring her under the law.

"The complexion of those who have been poisoned by *ku* becomes more than ordinarily beautiful. The *T'ien chi* (probably leaders among the women) look at them and smile. Then the victim must kowtow to a chieftaness and beg for the antidote. She will give the victim a pill. If the victim takes it, he instantly vomits strange things with human heads and the bodies of snakes, or having eight feet and six wings. These creatures cannot be killed with the sword, or burned. But if alum is placed on them, they die at once. Otherwise they will return to their old place. I lived long among these people, and know the prescription. Use *san Ch'i* (literally, three seven) powder and water-chestnuts to make pills. Add alum and tea leaves, making them into a powder. Take five *chien* with spring water. If vomiting follows, then stop. An old prescription says to take white *Jang-ho* and drink its juice, then sleep on the roots, after calling aloud the name of the witch. But the effect of this process is very slow."

The *T'ung Ch'i hsien chih*[1] says, "If the mat of the victim is burned, he will see for himself who the sorcerer is. The *ku* is a spirit, and goes out in the night to snatch the souls of the dead. The houses of *ku* sorcerers are very clean, because the ghosts of those who have been killed by the *ku* poison act as servants in them. If a man sits in a posture resembling the written word 'woman' (i.e. cross-legged), the *ku* cannot harm him. Or if the witch is enchanting a man, and he buries some of her food secretly under the intersection of two streets, the *ku* spirit will turn on the witch herself. And the *ku* spirit is filled with fear of the hedgehog. If a hedgehog is brought to the house of a witch, the *ku* will be caught immediately. All these prescriptions

---

[1]　洞溪纤志, chüan 2. By 陆次云. The author flourished under K'ang-hsi, 1662-1723. A book about the aboriginal tribes of Southwest China.

and methods of detecting *ku* have been tested and shown to be effective, so I publish them here."

The *Tien nan hsin yü*[1] in another passage remarks, "In Szechuan there are many who keep *ku*, especially the *chin-tsan*, which is the most malignant form. When the owner has become rich, and has the means, he sends it away.... There is no *chin-tsan ku* among the East and West Yi of Yunnan, but the mischief caused by mice, snake, and food *ku* is comparatively greater. On calm nights, when the clouds are heavy, there are things which glitter like meteors, sweeping low over the roofs and flying quickly. The long, luminous tail affects the eye and heart like cold flames. I was very much astonished. When I asked my fellow officials, I began to realize that the lights were due to *ku*, which had been let out by the inhabitants. They also told me that the *ku* was apt to eat children's brains. It also kidnapped spirits. In those families which kept *ku*, the women were always debauched by the *ku*. If the spirit were dissatisfied, it would turn on the keeper and eat his children. Then it could not be sent away until the keeper had become poor, and all his family had perished. For this reason people are often afraid to keep it. Moreover, keeping it is prohibited by law. So the practice is gradually dying out, but it still exists. Those who still supply themselves with *ku*, do so cretely. In Hsin-hsing and Chien-ch'uan I tried several times to discover who the sorcerers were, in order to put an end to such malevalent things.

---

[1] See p.1061, note [1].

Sometimes informants appeared, but no evidence could be secured. Hedgehogs are used in detecting *ku*, but without much effect. During the time that the suspects were under arrest, the flitting of the *ku* was noticeably less."

The *Shu yi chi* [1] says, "When Sun Hsin-yai of Shih-men was magistrate of K'a-hua (in Yunnan), he was once sitting in the hall when he noticed a kind of light flitting about like a meteor. He asked his servants what it was. They said that it was the flying *ku*, or snake *ku*. The family who serve the poisonous spirit become rich, but the women and girls of the family are debauched by the snake. The snake goes out every night, flitting like a meteor. When it comes to a less populous place, it comes down and eats the brains of men. So the inhabitants of K'ai-hua dare not sit outside after dark, being afraid of the *ku*."

The same work remarks again,[2] "The witch who cultivates *ku* must first take an oath before the spirit that she is willing not to be human in coming transmigrations, and will desire wealth in the present life only. When the victims of the poison die, their property is all removed (by supernatural power) to the house of the witch, and the ghost of the victim becomes her slave. All the work, ploughing, spinning and serving, is done by the enslaved spirit.... Those who have been poisoned by *ku* may cure

---

[1] 述异记, chüan 2.

[2] Ibid.

themselves by jumping into a dung pool. Yu-Ch'i , Yung-an, Sha-hsien, and other districts of Fukien all have *ku*."

"Recently magistrate Wang, of Yu-Ch'i, bought a load of melons. He opened the melons the next day, and all contained *ku* insects. He accused the man who had sold them, who in turn said that they were bought in a certain shop. The magistrate arrested the shopkeeper and questioned him. He said that he and his family had never been sorcerers. On being beaten, he admitted that there was a sorcerer who had a personal animosity against him. The sorcerer was arrested, and did not deny the accusation. The magistrate had him tortured, but he did not feel the pain. He was put in jail, but escaped during the night. He was followed to his house, but the whole family were gone.

"In recent years there was a strange man who taught others a method for curing *ku*. The man would go to the home of the witch, carrying a chicken. The witch would understand, and give him a dose of medicine. All this must be done silently. The medicine was a sure cure.

"In Fukien, there is toad *ku*, somewhat similar to the *chin-tsan ku*. Those who serve it are mostly covetous of the riches that accompany it. People sometimes see large sums of money and silks lying beside the road, and they understand that this is someone sending away the *ku*. The *ku* spirit follows anyone who takes the valuables. With the wealth, the sender leaves a book telling the methods of serving the *ku*. The one who picks up the *ku* must clean his house and worship the *ku* spirit only, forsaking all Buddhist and Taoist deities. On the day that belongs to metal, the *ku* spirit will excrete dung like that of white birds, which can be used as poison. Poisons are laid only on the days *keng-hsin* and *sheng-yu*. Those who are poisoned, first sneeze. Then the worms enter the intestines and all the joints. The victim loses consciousness, and his belly swells. When the worms have eaten his bones and entrails, he dies."

"The *ku* poison can be administered in drink as well as in food, or sprinkled on the collars and clothes of the victims. It can be laid on chickens, geese, fish, meat, fruits and vegetables. When a living chicken has been bewitched by *ku*, its legs are eaten by worms, but it can walk and cackle as usual. When meat is bewitched, it will not become soft on being cooked. In all food that has been bewitched, worms will germinate overnight. So the officials in this land will use food presented by others only when it has stood overnight. Food which has no worms on the second day is not bewitched. The spirits of those who have died of *ku* poison become the slaves of the witch. The witches sacrifice eggs to the *ku* spirit on the last night of the year. Husband and wife worship with naked bodies, and thus square their accounts with the *ku* spirit. When a servant of the Yamen is poisoned, the sorcerer gives five ounces of silver to the *ku*; for all official, he gives fifty ounces. Those who poison more people, acquire greater riches. If a sorcerer becomes tired of the *ku*, he doubles the original amount of money he picked up with the *ku* in order to send it away." [1]

Yüan Mei[2] says, "Almost all families in Yunnan keep *ku*. It can excrete gold and silver, so they get rich because of it. They let the *ku* out every night, and it darts about like lightning, spreading eastward and westward. A great noise causes it to fall. It may be a snake, toad, or any kind of insect or reptile. People conceal their children because they are afraid of their being eaten by the *ku*. This *ku* is kept in a secret room, and is fed by the women. The *ku* is injured if it is seen by men, because it is formed of pure *Yin* (the female principle of the universe). That *ku* which devours men will excrete gold, while that which devours women will excrete silver. All this was told me by Hua Feng, the general formerly commanding in Yunnan."

Again, in the same work:[3]"Chu Yi-jen was an expert calligraphist, and Ch'en Hsi-fang, the prefect of Ch'ing-yüan in Knangsi, employed him as secretary. One hot summer day, the prefect invited his colleagues to a feast. As they removed their hats on sitting down to the table, they saw a large frog sitting on the top of Chu's head. They brushed it away, when the frog fell to the ground and disappeared. They feasted until night, and again the frog crept to the top of Chu's head, without his being aware of it.They drove it away from him once more, and it fell on the table, spoilt the food, and

---

[1]   Ibid.

[2]   袁枚. A.D. 1715-97. A voluminous writer of the Manchu period. This passage is taken from his 子不语, chüan 14. A book recording supernatural events.

[3]   Ibid, ehiian 19. The passage is quoted by De Groot, p. 852.

disappeared."

"When Chu returned to his room, the top of his head itched. The next day his hair fell out, and his head swelled like a red tumour. Suddenly the swelling burst, and a frog stuck its head out. Its forefeet rested on the top of Chu's head, but the lower part of the frog was in the tumour. He picked it with a needle, but could not kill it. He tried to pull it out, but the pain was unbearable. The physicians did not know how to cure it. Finally an old gate-keeper said that it was the *ku*. On his advice they pierced it with a gold hair-pin, and the frog died. Chu had no further trouble, but the top of his skull sank down like a bowl."

The *Ch'ien chi* [1] says, "The Miao women who kept *ku* got plenty of money. When the *ku* becomes too strong, it must be sent away. They do this sometimes as often as once a month. Those ignorant of this often pick up money or packages along the mountain paths. The *ku* follows them home. When it gets to the house, it must remain there several days. If its wants are not satisfied, it will cause calamity. During the fall, the Miao women carry pears in cloth bags, selling the pears to children. Many children are poisoned by *ku* in this way. This was discovered by some of the children, and so now, when they buy pears, they ask, 'Do you have *ku* poison in your pears? ' If the reply is ' No,' the children are safe. Among the women of the Shan, there

---

① 黔记, chüan 32. By 李宗昉. Written about the beginning of the 19th Cent. It describes the province of Kueichou.

are many who keep *ku*."

In the *Fan t'ien lu tsung t'an* [①] is the following passage. "Recently a man named Chiang ch'an-p'o reported that in the district of Lu-an *ku* is used to kill people. The house of the witch is always clean, since the work is done by the *ku*. Many inn-keepers serve the *ku*. If an inn-keeper and his inn are exceptionally clean, those who stay there overnight are poisoned. During one night, several travellers simply disappeared, and all their money and baggage came into the hands of the inn-keeper. There was no sign of the corpses because they were entirely eaten by the *ku* worms."

"Travellers in this district must know whether the inn contains *ku*. They lay their luggage at random on the ground, close the door, and stand outside for a while. If no servants appear, and yet the baggage has 〔mysteriously〕 been arranged in order, they know that this inn has *ku*. The traveller must not speak of this openly,but pays his fee and goes to some other inn. Such travellers will not be injured by the keeper of the inn, but will be regarded as men with a great destiny."

The *Yi chien chih pu* [②] says, "In the various districts of Fukien, there are many *Ku* poisoners, but they are especially prevalent in the districts of Ku-T'ien and Ch'ang-Ch'i. There are four kinds, snake *ku*, *chin tsan ku*, centipede *ku*, and frog *ku*. All can change their forms, and become invisible.

---

① 梵天庐谈丛, chüan 33. By 柴萼. A work of miscellaneous notes, published by the Chung-hua Book Co. of shanghai in 1926.

② 夷坚志补, chüan 23.

All have males and females, which copulate at fixed intervals, varying from two months to once in two years. When the date arrives, the family which keeps the *ku* prepares a ceremony to welcome their coming, and a basin of water is placed before them. The male and female appear in the water and copulate. Then the poison floats on the water, and can be collected with a needle. A person must be poisoned on this date. This is the breath of Yin and Yang (the male and female principles of the universe), and it is infused into people's stomachs, symbolic of the genital functions. It is not effective overnight. When a guest arrives, even a relative, he is poisoned. The poison can be placed in food, drink, or medicine, but it cannot be put into hot soup. When the medium is too hot, the poison is ineffective. If no outsiders come in on that day, a member of the family is selected to be poisoned. When the poison first enters the stomach the victim feels nothing, but gradually the *ku* worms generate and feed on the victim's blood. The worms grow, reproduce, and consume the internal organs. The pain becomes unbearable, and can be relieved only temporarily by drinking water boiled a hundred times. As the pain becomes worse, the victims groan and scratch the bed. When the victim is dying, several hundred worms come out of his eyes, nose, ears and mouth. If they are dried, they can become alive again, even after a long time. The ghost of the victim is controlled by the *ku*, just as the tiger enslaves the

*Ch'ang,*① and becomes a slave of the family. Such 〔an enslaved〕 spirit cannot be reincarnated. Even if the corpse of the victim is cremated, the heart and lungs will not burn, but will look like honeycombs."

"In 1175, the mother of Lin Sao-shuan of Ku-T'ien (her surname was Huang) lay dying, apparently from poison. The members of the family said that if she had been poisoned by *ku*, and her matrix was burned so that the light of the fire would shine upon her, she would reveal who had poisoned her. They did this, and she said that on a certain date, she had been poisoned while eating by Huang Ku's wife, Lai Shih. The demon was still in their kitchen. Lin Sao shuan reported this to the local magistrate, and they went to the house of Huang Ku. In the kitchen they found some pieces of silver, five colored thread, jewels, and small wooden figures on which were written five "Yi" and five "Shun" (words meaning "opposed" and "favorable"). These were in a box with seven holes. There were also two packs of needles, each fifty in number, and eleven needles were without eyes. All these were not things ordinarily used by people. The man was accused before the magistrate. The magistrate arrested Huang Ku, who feigned death in the court. When released, he became alive again, as if helped by some supernatural power."

"Yü Ch'ing of Kuei chi was judge at that time, and when the prefect

---

① 伥.The spirit of a person who has been eaten by a tiger. It urges the tiger to murder others, in accordance with a common belief that the soul of a murdered man may return to earth if a substitute is provided.

ordered him to examine the case, Huang Ku behaved in the same way. Yü Ch'ing was angry and afraid that the criminal would escape the law, so he came down and cut off Huang's head. He put the head in a basket, and reported the act to the prefect. The prefect reported the case to the emperor and a higher judge, Hsieh Ssu chi, was asked to investigate the case."

"Hsich accompanied the local officials to the house of Huang Ku, where he saw centipedes of unusual size. Hsieh said, 'This is the evidence.' Lai Shih was arrested, and tried by Hsieh himself. After a three days trial, the death penalty was passed upon her. The figures (she confessed) were used in divination. If the response was favorable, the guest was poisoned; if unfavorable, a member of the family. The eyeless needles were used in gathering the poison, and the number showed that eleven persons had been poisoned. The *ku* likes to eat silk brocade, but if this could not be procured, the five colored threads were fed to it instead. The silver was to have been used in sending the *ku* away.... Huang Ku's criminal acts really reached Heaven, and Yü Ch'ing obliterated an evil-doer by killing him. Many scholars wrote poems in praise of him."

There are also a number of stories indicating that the virtuous scholar need not fear *ku*. The Chinese have a proverb which says that the heretic cannot overcome the righteous man. Among the Chinese, the educated men have always been the backbone of the moral system. It is natural to find that such men can repel evil influences.

An interesting case is recorded in the *Mu fu yen hsien lu* of Pi Chung-hsün [①] "In Chih-chou there was a scholar named Tsou Lang, having a *chin-shih* degree. He was poor, but of upright character. One day he was about to start for a nearby town, when on opening his door in the early morning, he saw lying beside it a basket. He opened the basket, and found that it was filled with silver wine-vessels and about a hundred ounces of silver. As it was early morning, no one was watching him. The scholar took it in and said to his wife, 'These things came to me unexpectedly. Are they given to me by Heaven?' He had scarcely finished speaking, when he saw on his left thigh something that wiggled in a shimmer of gold. It was a caterpillar. He picked it off with his hand. His hand was hardly turned, when it was back in its old place. He trampled on the worm with his foot and smashed it, but immediately it was again on his body. He threw it into water and into fire, cut it with his sword, and hacked it with an axe, without avail. It followed him everywhere, and never left him. Tsou Lang finally asked the advice of his friends. Those who knew about such matters told him,"

"'You have been betrayed. This thing is the *chin tsan*. Although it is small, it will cause a great calamity. It can enter the belly and ruin the intestines, after which it will come out unharmed.'"

"Tsou Lang became still more frightened, and told his friend about finding the basket."

---

① 幕府燕闲录, extracted in 说郛, chüan 14. By 毕中询. A lost work of the Sung period.

"His friend said, 'I knew that already. If you serve this *ku*, you will become rich quickly. This worm eats four inches of Shu satin every day. Collect its excretion, dry it, and grind it to powder. Put a little in food and drink, and give these to others. Anyone who takes it will surely be poisoned. The worm will get what it desires, and it will remove the valuables of its victims to your house.'"

"Tsou Lang laughed and said, 'Am I the man to do this? '

"His friend said, 'I know surely that you do not desire to do it, but what other thing can you do? '"

"Tsou Lang replied, 'I shall put this worm into the basket with the other things and carry it away. Then there will be no further trouble.'"

"'When a man serves this worm long enough,' the friend said, 'he will become rich. Then he gives several times the amount he originally found with the *ku* away. This is called finding the *chin-tsan* a husband. Then the *ku* worm will go. But if you put in only what you found with the worm, I am sure it will not go. Now you are poor. How can you give several times more than you found? I am really concerned about you.'"

"Tsou Lang looked at the sky, and replied, 'During my whole life I have tried to be an upright man. I swore not to lose my virtue. It is my misfortune that this thing has happened to me.' He went home and told his wife, saying, 'It is impossible for me to serve the *ku* worm. I am too poor to send it away. The only thing left for me is death. You had better prepare for the future.'"

"He put the worm into his mouth and swallowed it. His family tried to stop him, but it was too late. His wife wept bitterly, thinking that he would surely die. But after a few days he had no further trouble, eating and drinking as usual. A month passed, and still he was not affected. He finally died at a ripe age. And by means of the silver he had found in the basket, he became well-to-do. Is it that the sincerity of a man can overcome the most poisonous influences?"

The following account is taken from the *Yi chien san chih*.[1]

"In the district of Ch'ang-chou there was a brave scholar of strong character. He often thought that while men were cowardly, there was nothing worthy of being dreaded. He regretted that there were no evil spirits to interfere with him and test his courage. Once he went with a few friends to another village, and saw a parcel covered with silk on the ground. The others dared not even look at it, but he laughed and said, 'I am poor, why should I not take it?'"

"He opened it before them, and found several rolls of silk, three large pieces of silver, and a *ku* frog. He said to the frog, 'You may go where you wish; what I want is the silk and the silver.' He took the things home, where his family wept bitterly, thinking that a calamity would soon occur. The scholar said to them, 'This concerns me, not you.'"

---

① 夷坚三志壬, chüan 4. A work of the Sung period.

"That night when he went to bed, there were two frogs, as big as a year old baby, occupying his bed. He killed and ate them both. His family again lamented, but he was delighted to get such good meat. Then he proceeded to get drunk, fell asleep, and passed a peaceful night. The next night there appeared more than ten frogs, though smaller than before. Again he cooked and ate them. The next night there were thirty. Night after night the frogs were increasingly numerous, but their size became ever smaller. At last the whole house was full of frogs, and it was impossible to eat them all. He hired men to bury them in the wilderness. Yet his courage was strengthened still more. Finally the thing stopped after a month, so he laughed and said, 'Is the calamity caused by *ku* no more than this ?' His wife asked him to buy hedgehogs as a precaution but he said,' I am the hedgehog; what other do you want? ' His family was pacified, and nothing untoward happened. So other people commended his behavior."

The *Yi chien chih pu* contains the following story: [1]"In the city of ch'uan chou, there was a house tenanted by several families. One of the tenants was an under-official named Lin, a native of Ch'in. One night he found an old bamboo basket lying at the street end of an alley. He kicked it playfully, and a small embroidered blanket fell out. On opening it, he discovered silver vessels worth more than two hundred tales. As there was no one around, he took the things home, thinking they had been given to

---

[1]　夷坚志补, chüan 23.

him by Heaven."

"All his neighbors were astonished by this, and the landlord said, 'This is the Ming custom of serving the *chin-tsan*. The original owner has become rich, and wanted to shift the calamity to others. Since you have taken this bait, you must not regret it. Today a demon will appear to you. You had better welcome and serve it. Otherwise, great misfortune will happen to you.' Lin remained silent."

"That night a snake, ten feet long, crawled in as if much pleased. Lin caught it and said, ' Are you the demon of the *chin-tsan* ? I cannot please you by poisoning people to enrich myself. If I do not, I shall be eaten by you. There is only one death, but I would rather eat you first.' So he bit the snake, and swallowed it from head to tail, not even leaving the bones. Then he called for wine, and drank until he fell asleep. Next morning he rose up well and unharmed, and later he became well-to-do. All admired his courage."

There is an amusing story of this sort in the *Fan T'ien lu t'an tsung.*[①] "An old man named Tseng, of Lung-yen in Fukien, picked up a box from the road. On opening it, he found about twenty ounces of silver. He took it home. During the night, a handsome young man appeared to him, who tried to compel him to burn incense and take an oath before Heaven that he would

---

① 梵天庐谈丛, chüan 33.By 柴萼.A work of miscellaneous notes,published by the Chung hua Book Co.of shanghai in 1926.

administer poison to someone on a certain date. The old man realized that it was the spirit of the *chin-tsan*. He refused the request, and so the spirit continued to trouble him. Finally worn out, he faithfully promised. On the fatal day, his son-in-law came. The spirit secretely put the poison in the food, and when the son-in-law returned home, he had violent pains in his abdomen. The old man realized that the pains were due to the poison, and relieved him by administering an antidote. The spirit was very angry, and complained to Tseng."

"The old man replied, 'He is my son-in-law, and my daughter has no children. How can I poison him ?'"

"The spirit came another time, and exacted a similar promise. This time his sister's son came. The nephew also became violently ill on returning home, and the old man cured him. That night the spirit greatly annoyed Tseng, and the whole family had no sleep."

"The old man Tseng said to the spirit, 'My sister was widowed when she was very young, and this son is her only child. If he dies from poison, my sister's descendants will be cut off. Moreover, I am not willing to do such things. Let us talk the matter over now. Suppose I give you back the original amount of silver, on condition that you go to someone else ?'"

"'Since I came to your house,' replied the spirit, 'your farm produce has increased every day, and you forget about this benefit. You have not poisoned anyone yet, and you want me to go. You must add at least thirty percent interest to the sum you give me. Otherwise I will not spare you.'"

"Then the old man took count, and calculated that he must give the spirit two hundred and more ounces of silver. He got the silver by selling his farm. Then he put it into the box, which he left where he had originally found it."

This ends the collection of illustrations of the practice of *ku*, a collection covering the entire period of Chinese literature. A few generalizations may be made in conclusion.

It must not be supposed, as De Groot implies, that all Chinese believe in these things. On the contrary, the fact that it was extremely difficult to make this collection of passages is in itself evidence of the opposite. The physical symptoms ascribed to magical causes are not imaginary, and the diseases are very real. *Ku* figures largely in Chinese medical works, and the term is still used to describe certain conditions caused by internal parasites.

The idea of *ku* is very old. It probably originated in the idea that disease was sometimes caused by black magic. The use of the word as a divination symbol, and in the other ways mentioned in classic literature, are probably later accretions. The concept appears peculiar to Eastern Asia, at least in the method of producing the *Ku* by allowing poisonous things to eat each other. At the same time, all sorts of extraneous notions have been added from time to time.

The practice appears to be a connecting link between Chinese culture and the cultures of Southeastern Asia. However, it was early suppressed in China proper, and survived among the aboriginal tribes of the south.

[与 J.K. Shryock 合作,

原载 *Journal of the American Oriental Society*, Vol.55(1935),pp.1-30]

THE ORIGIN OF YÜ HUANG[①]

Yü Huang, sometimes translated Jade Emperor or Pearly Emperor, is the supreme deity of the Taoist Pantheon. Historically he is a late figure and does not play a prominent rôle in literary sources before the Sung period (A.D. 960- 1279), but from the standpoint of popular Chinese mythical lore he is undoubtedly one of the most important deities and his origin should be carefully studied.

The Taoist version of his origin, that he was the son of the king and queen of the country of Kuang-yên-miao yüeh 光严妙乐, a non-existant utopia, should be repudiated as a late rationalization after the pattern of the

---

①   The author desires to express his gratitude to Prof. Elisséeff for correetions and suggestions and Dr. J. K. Shryock for improvement in English.

life of Buddha. [1]

On the other hand the statement of some scholars that the god is a fabrication of the Sung emperor Chên tsung (真宗, A.D. 998-1022) cannot be sustained. This misconception may be due to Wieger [2] and has probably been followed by others who have dealt with Chinese mythology, such as Doré, [3] Couling, [4] Werner, [5] Ferguson, [6] etc. It is not likely that an emperor who wished to cover up his defeat at the hands of barbarians by some divine ordinance would invent a deity totally unknown to his subject, [7] Maspero has said that "... with false visions even more than genuine ones it is essential to base them upon well established belief..."and "it is evident that, for the

---

[1]　*Kao-shang Yü Huang Pên Hsing Chi Ching* 高上玉皇本行集经，Commercial Press ed. *Tao tsang* 道藏，23, chüan 上【盈一】4-6. The date of composition of this work is not definitely known; generally attributed to the Southern Sung (A.D. 1128-1279) or early Yüan (A.D. 1280-1367) periods. For a translation of this legend, see Lewis HODOUS, *Folkways in China* (London,1929), 28-31.

[2]　Léon WIEGER, *Textes historques 1* (1902), 1842 and 1846.

[3]　Henri DORÉ, *Recherches sur les superstitions en Chine* (1915) 9, 468 472.

[4]　Samuel COULING, *The Encyclopaedia Sinica* (1917) 619.

[5]　E. T. C. WERNER, *Myths and Legends of china* (1922) 130-131; and *A Dictionary of Chinese Mythology* (1932) 598-611.

[6]　J. C. FERGUSON, *Chinese Mythology* (in *Mythology of all Races*, vol. 8) (1928)58-59.
The works of early writers concerning this subject are disregarded in this paper as most of them are so erroneous that they are hardly worth correction. e.g., H. C. DUBOSE, *The Dragon, Image, and Demon* (1887), 384, says:"As a matter of history, the Emperor Hwéi Tsung in the twelfth century conferred upon a magician, by the name of Chang Ye, the title of Shang te, the Pearly Emperor, and the people, finding one deity so much simpler than an abstract triumvirate, accepted him as their Optimus Maximus."

[7]　The evidence these authors adduce is very flimsy. The only work they refer to is the *T'ung Chien Kang Mu*, more accurately *T'ung Chien Kang Mu Hsü Pien* 通鉴纲目续编, as the *Kang Mu* proper ends with the year A.D. 959. Doré (op. cit., 471, note 1) refers to Wieger, Couling follows Doré. Werner and Ferguson refer directly to the *T'ung Chien Kang Mu* but do not give any exact reference. Actually they all use Wieger without consulting the *T'ung chien Kang Mu Hsü Pian*, because there is nothing in the text and annotations to justify the statement that Chên-tsung invented Yü Huang.

Emperor to have so definite a vision of his ancestor bringing him the order from the god, the god must already have ranked as a supreme deity in popular belief."① But Maspero went no farther than the other authors in

Wieger says in his Textes historiques (p. 1842), "En 1012, date mémorable, invention du dieu le plus populaire de la Chine moderne. Laissons parler l'Histoire.... "Then follows a translation of a passage from the *T'ung Chien Kang Mu Hsü Pien* [*cf.* 清嘉庆九年 (1804), 苏州聚文堂刊本 ch. 3, 59b] in which only the name Yü Huang is mentioned and nothing is said of invention.On page 1846 of the same work Wieger remarks again: "<u>A</u> cette occasion, la Grande Histoire renferme la note très importante que voui:' C'est ici que commence l'histoire du *Pur Auguste*. On ne salt absolument rien de ce personnage, inconnu auparavant. Sa légende, telle que la postédté la débite, fut, selon toute apparence, confectionée à cette date." The original of this passage is given by Wieger as follows: 按祀典之称玉皇，始此，而本末未详. 近世所奉玉皇本行集经,或始于此时也 .This annotation does not occur in the text of the *T'ung Chien Kang Mu Hsü Pien*, nor in the *Sung Shih* 宋史 nor in the *Yü p'i T'unng Chien Kang Mu Hsu Pien*, nor in the *T'ung Chien Chi Lan*, nor in the *Hsü Tzǔ Chih T'ung Chien*, nor in the *Sung Shih Chi-shih Pên Mo*. I do not know which work is meant by the term 'Grande Histoire'. Nevertheless, Wieger's rendering is inaccurate and misleading. <u>A</u> more literal translation of his text would run as follows: "The use of the title Yü Huang in state sacrificial and worshipping ceremonies 祀典 commences from here but his whole history is not clear. The *Yü Huang Pên Hsing Chi Ching* used nowadays probably dates from this time." It is very clear that this note says nothing about the invention of Yü Huang at this time but only that the state worship of him began from here. Wieger's interpretation that "Le 玉皇 Pur Auguste, le dieu le plus populaire de la Chine méridionale moderne, fut bel et bien inventé à cette époque..." (op.cit., 1846, note) is entirely unwarranted.

The recognition of Yü Huang by the state religion was primarily connected with the *T'ien Shu* incident, 天书 'Ecrite C'élestes ' of Chên-Tsung's reign. After the conclusion of the truce of Shan Yüan 澶渊 with the Khitan 契丹, which the Emperor later considered humiliating, he conspired to gain prestige among his subjects by some supernatural ordinance. He turned visionary and received the *T'ien Shu* from heaven. This further led the Emperor to perform the *Fêng Shan* 封禅 ceremonies, which could only be performed, theoretically, by founders of dynasties and successful great emperors. The *T'ien Shu Fêng Ssǔ* 天书封祀 was one of the most important and preposterous events during Chên-Tsung's reign and the documents concerning the whole affair were summarized in CH'ÊN Pangchan 陈邦瞻, *Sung Shih Chi Shih Pên Mo* 宋史纪事本末 22.

① 　Henri MASPERO, *Mythologie de la Chine moderne, Mythologie asiatique illustrée* (Paris, 1928) 239-248. The quotation is from the English translation (London, 1932), pp. 263-271.

'Chen tsong' of the French edition should read 'Tchen tsong' according to the romanization used in Maspero's work. *Chen tsong* 神宗 (Shên tsung for us)was the Sung emperor who reigned A.D. 1068-1085. Correspondingly the '*Shên tsung*'in the English translation should read ' Chên-tsung' .

I take this occasion to ask M. Maspero on what authority he calls Fig. 10, p. 248 (Fig. 12, p. 272 in the English tr.) "La déesse de la Lune." Chinese artists seldom represent female figures showing their breasts except in obscene scenes. Fig. 10, so far as I can see, is not feminine at all. If the string of "gold cash" 金钱 were not missing, it would be the Liu Hai Hsi Ch'an 刘海戏蟾. [EDITORS' NOTE: Cf. V. ALEKSEEV, Les doubles immortels et le taoiste au crapaud d'or auompagnant le dieu de la richesse, *Rscueil du musée d'anthropologie et d'ethno graphie de l'Academie des Sciences 5* (Petrograd, 1918), 253-318].

tracing the early evidence of the development of this myth.

Hodous traced the name of Yü Huang to the *Book of Changes*[①]. This, however, is a little too imaginative.[②] He also cited the *T'ien kung*, heavenly lord, in the *Sou Shên Chi* 搜神记 [③] and the *T'ien Kung* "venerable old man of heaven," Chang Chien, in the *Yu yang tsa tsu* as possible precursors of Yü Huang. As to the *T'ien kung*, it is so vague that it can be interpreted in many ways. The legend of Chang Chien in the *Yu yang tsa tsu* [④] bears certain resemblances to the myth of Chang Têng-lai which will be given later in this paper, but he also cannot be considered as the precursor of Yü Huang, because the term Yü Huang had already become well known in literary sources almost half a century before the composition of the *Yu yang tsa tsu*.[⑤] Thus it is inconceivable that Tuan Ch'êng-shih should use such a vague term as *T'ien wêng*, "venerable old man of heaven," if he meant Yü Huang.

---

① 　Hodous, op. cit. 26.

② 　周易，说卦："乾为天，为圜，为君，为父，为玉，为金，为寒，为水，为大赤，为良马，为老马，为瘠马，为驳马，为木果."十三经注疏本, chüan 12, pp. 8-9.

　　Hodous does not give any exact reference, but I suppose this is the passage he referred to. If he interprets "Ch'ien is heaven...ruler...jade..." as Yü Huang, then how would he interpret "Ch'ien is...old horse..." ?

③ 　Hodous, op. cit., 27. Hodous did not give any exact reference to the *Sou Shên Chi*. So far as I can find, the term *T'ien kung* 天公 occurs only twice in one place in ch. 10. lb. The term *T'ien ti* 天帝, heavening emperor, also occurs in this work (ch. 19. 2) but it is used with the same vague meaning as in the case of *T'ien kung*.

④ 　酉阳杂俎，四部丛刊本，14.2.天翁张坚.

⑤ 　Hodous says (op. cit. 27), "In the *Yu yang tsa tsu*, written at the end of the eighth century ..." This date is too early. The author Tuan Ch'êng-shih 段成式 died in the year A.D. 863. His birth date is not known but it cannot be much earlier than A.D. 790 because his father Tuan Wên-ch'ang 段文昌, was born in 773 and died in 831. From his biography in the *Old T'ang History* 旧唐书167. 9 it would seem that the *Yu yang tsa tsu* was most probably composed during his later years, possibly around the middle oi the ninth century. The *Yu yang tsa tsu* itself records facts as late as 840.

The earliest occurrence of the name Yü Huang is found in the works of the Confucian scholar Han Yü (A.D. 768-824). In a poem admiring the plum blossoms,[1] he wrote:

"Riding clouds we come together to the home of Yü Huang."

Riding clouds is a mode of locomotion characteristic of Chinese gods and immortals. Liu Tsung-yüan (A.D. 773-819), the great T'ang essayist and poet, in a poem about a waterfall,[2] wrote:

"Suddenly it is like coming to the presence of Yü Huang,
The jade pendants upon the front of his heavenly crown hanging down?"
The author was comparing the sparkling waterfall to the lustrous jade tassels of Yü Huang's crown. It suggests a well developed myth to which the poet was alluding. More specific was the poet Yüan Chên 元稹 (A. D. 779-831). Bragging about his newly acquired residence to Po Chü-i (A.D. 772-846), he wrote: [3]

"I am the petty official in charge of Yü Huang's incense table,

Although banished, I can still live in P'êng-lai."

P'êng lai was the legendary island of the immortals. All these poetical quotations should be understood in a metaphorical sense. Chinese poetry is noteworthy for its conciseness. From these few lines the picturesque figure of Yü Huang can be clearly visualized. The T'ang dynasty (A.D. 618-907)

---

① 昌黎先生集，蟫隐庐影宋世綵堂本，5.3.

② 柳河东集，四部备要本，42.14,界围岩水帘诗. "忽如朝玉皇，天冕垂前旒."

③ 元氏长庆集，四部丛刊本，22.2,以州宅夸乐天. "我是玉皇香案吏，谪居犹得住蓬来."

was the great period of Chinese poetry, and it is natural to find important material embodied in poetic form. The frequent occurrence of Yü Huang in the poetry of this period shows the great popularity of the myth and the poetical nature of the theme.

Somewhat later there was a well known painting of the imaginary court scene of Yü Huang by the famous artist Shih K'o 石恪 of the Kingdom of Shu 蜀 (A.D. 908-965). The painting has probably been lost, but a full description of it has been handed down to us in the critical catalogue, *Tê Yü chai Hua p'in.*[1] It says:

"A picture of the court ceremony of Yü Huang by Shih K'o of Shu. The T'ien-hsien, Ling-kuan, Chin-T'ung, Yü nü, San knan, T'ai-i, Ch'i-yüan, Ssǔ-shêng, Ching-wei,[2] gods of stars, wind, rain, thunder, lightning, lords of the mountains and lakes, deities ruling above and below the earth, etc., are all gathered at the court of the Emperor. The great heavenly Emperor Yü Huang sits facing south with all due decorum and dignity. All the deities look up to his pure lustrous countenance with raised heads. Those who see this picture will feel the exaltation and animation. It is like placing oneself

---

[1]　德隅斋画品 by Li Chai 李廌 of the Sung dynasty. 顾氏文房小说本，p.7-8. 玉皇朝会图.
[2]　天仙，灵官，金童，玉女，三官，太一，七元，四圣，经纬.

in the T'ung Ming Tien.[①]

"Shih K'o's temperament is unrestrained, humorous and satirical. Therefore his paintings are unruly and often go beyond the ordinary rules, but they do not lose their unusual beauty. So of the figures he has painted here, some are extraordinarily ugly or mysteriously crabbed in order to insinuate the unusual 〔gathering〕. The deities of the waters have crabs or fishes suspended to their waists 〔a feature he intended〕 to show disdain for the onlookers.... In this painting he dared not blaspheme the figure of Yü Huang, but still it is not free from amusing implications intending to obtain laughter from admirers 〔of the picture〕."

The vividness of the description and the reverent language of the critic toward Yü Huang combine to show his importance as a supreme deity.

All these citations show that Yü Huang was much earlier than the time of the emperor Chên tsung. He only utilized a well known, popular deity to further his cause. But through his imperial patronage Yü Huang gained state recognition and became more important in popular religious beliefs than ever before.

Yü Huang as a high god dates back to the eighth and nineth centuries

---

① 通明殿 Palace of penetrating illumination,i.e. the palace of yü Huang. Cf *I shêng Pao tê Chuan* 翊圣保德传 by WANG Ch'in-jo 王钦若(died 1024) of the Sung dynasty (道藏，1006册，卷中，Ia⁶-b⁴)：守真尝朝礼至玉皇大殿，睹其额曰通明殿，不晓其旨.因焚香告曰：通明之谊，窃所未喻，敢祈真教？真君曰：上帝在无上三天，为诸天之尊，万象群仙，无不臣者.常升金殿，金殿之光明，照于帝身，身之光明，照于金殿.光明通彻，无所不照，故为通明殿.This is the earliest explanation of the meaning of T'ung Ming Tien.

A.D., and his actual genesis may be still a few centuries earlier, ① but the actual condition of his origin and the details of the myth are still shrouded in mystery, and as in the case of most popular deities, may never be known. However, there is a popular version of this myth, which does not seem to have been recorded. This version is widely distributed over Central and West China, where the Taoist religion has had its fullest development from the time of Chang Lu.

According to this version, the surname of Yü Huang is Chang, and his first name is Têng-lai.② He is more or less an opportunist, a trickster, and obtained his throne by chance. The story is based on the *Fêng shên Chuan,* a novel describing the canonization of gods. This version continues the *Fêng Shên Chuan*, and since this is a well-known work, it is not necessary to recapitulate the whole story here,③ but only to start from the place where the Yü Huang myth is first mentioned.

Chiang T'ai-kung, standing on the Fêng Shên T'ai, Terrace of Canonization, ④ appointed all those who lost their lives during the bloody

---

① Prof. Elisséeff suggested to me that there might be a connection between Yü Huang and Yü Ching 玉京 mentioned in *Wei Shu* 魏书 114. 24b-25a, and in *Sui Shu* 隋书 35. 27b-28a (The paging is that of the 同文 edition). If this could be proved it would definitely carry the myth farther back three or four centuries. Cf. also J. R. WARE, The *Wei Shu* and the *Sui Shu* on Taoism, *JAOS* 53 (1933), 214 and 243.

② 张等来.

③ Those who are not familiar with the *Fêng shên Chuan* 封神传 or *Fêng Shên Yen-i* 封神演义, may see WERNER, *A Dictionary of Chiese Mythology* under Chiang Tzŭ-ya. A very brief account is given there. See also DORÉ, op. cit. (note 4), IX, pp. 665-670. This novel is partially translated and resumed by Wilhelm GRUBE and Herbert MUELIER in *Fêng-Shên-Yen-i, Die Metamorphosen der Goetter,* Leiden, 1912.

④ 封神台.

campaign against the Shang as gods to rule over the destinies of man. For a time the procedure was uneventful, but finally only the position of Yü Huang was left vacant, which Chiang T'ai-kung intended to reserve for himself. Some impatient bystander inquired of him who was to become Yü Huang. Half-heartedly, Chiang T'ai-kung replied, "Têng-lai." This literally meant, "I'm coming to that." Standing beside the Fêng Shên T'ai was the opportunist Chang Têng lai. On hearing his name called, he prostrated himself before the 'Terrace' and thanked Chiang T'ai kung for creating him Yü Huang. Stupefied by this unexpected turn of events, and unable to retract his words, Chiang T'ai-kung in his intense anger cursed Chang Têng-lai, saying: "Your sons will become thieves and your daughters prostitutes." Chang Têng-lai had, however, to become Yü Huang, because whatever Chiang T'ai-kung says must be fulfilled, for "his mouth is gold and his words jade."

Now there was no place left for Chiang T'ai-kung himself; the only shrine he could find for himself was the windowsills. Consequently, in present-day China, especially in Central China among the peasants, whenever there is a wedding or a child-birth, or any event that needs protection from malevolent spirits, an inscription is invariably pasted on the window of the room of the bride, or the laboring mother, saying: "Chiang T'ai-kung is here, all gods avoid." [1] The wedding night and childbirth are critical moments that have to be safeguarded against malevolent spirits. The

---

① 姜太公在此，诸神回避.

idea is that, although Chiang T'ai-kung lost his position as Yü Huang, he still has prestige among the gods because he canonized them, and because he is the only one who hovers around the windows. According to popular belief, evil spirits can only enter the house through the windows because the doors are guarded by door gods whose images are placed there and renewed every new year. If Chiang T'ai kung guards the windows, the house will be secure against all malevolent spirits.

Although Chang Têng-lai became Yü Huang, he could not annul the curse imposed upon him by Chiang T'ai-kung. So his sons became thieves, and after having committed many minor felonies, they planned a more daring attempt. They went to steal the precious lotus seat of the Buddha. This feat was impossible because they could not escape from the great power of the Buddha, who is omniscient and omnipotent. With a turn of his hand Buddha enslaved them under a pagoda and doomed them to remain there forever. This is why at the foot of every pagoda there are grotesque figures who seem to support it with great exertion. They are the sons of Chang Yü Huang. [1]

Yü Huang's daughters were doomed to be prostitutes. As their father was Yü Huang, they did not become prostitutes in the ordinary sense of the term, but all married men. There are a wealth of tales about these marriages

---

[1]　This explanation is certainly wrong. They are not Yü Huang's sons but guardian deities of the pagoda usually of the Vajrapāni type. For illustration, see G. ECKE and P. DEMIEVILIE, *The Twin Pagodas of Zayton* (Cambridge, Mass.,1935), pls. 12 and 14, fig. 5-6, etc. It shows, however, the imagination of the popular mind in seeking to explain what is not understood.

between immortals and mortals which are too long to be related here. The most dramatic, humorous, and entertaining is the marriage of Yü Huang's seventh daughter Chang Ch'i chieh, Chang the seventh sister, with the semi-imbecile Ts'ui Wên jui.① Wên-jui was a poor wretch clothed in rags, simple and ignorant. He was a wood cutter because he was too stupid to earn a living by any other work. Yet he was very filial and obedient to his aged and invalid mother. Every day he went to the woods to chop down a bundle of wood which he sold in the market in order to buy the necessary food for his mother. Day after day he went to the forest and cut the wood and nothing eventful happened. While contented with his lot, he really did not know what contentment meant. One day while he was chopping wood, Chang Ch'i chieh came to him and offered to marry him. Ts'ui Wên-jui was so stupid that he did not know what a wife was. The conversation between the two is the most humorous as well as the most ridiculous that anyone can imagine. Finally Wên-jui brought the matter to his mother. She refused on the ground that her son was too stupid to have such a beautiful wife. "It will be a great calamity instead of a great fortune." Chang Ch'i-chieh insisted and she pledged herself to be a good wife and to do all the cooking, weaving and housework. She would not leave unless Wên jui took her to wife. Finally the old lady yielded and they were married.

Actually Chang Ch'i-chieh proved to be a very good wife. She was

---

① 張七姐下凡嫁崔文瑞.

industrious and obedient. The cloth she wove was so beautiful and fine that no one would believe it was done with mortal hands. All went on very well. Unfortunately, one day when she was working outside, a rich and handsome young man of the district passed by and saw her. He was so infatuated by her beauty that he was willing to try any means to marry her. The mother-in-law was much perturbed because she was apprehensive of the danger involved, but the wife told her not to worry. She promised to marry this rich young man provided he would pay her husband Wên-jui an exorbitant bride-price to compensate for his loss of a beautiful wife. To this the young man gladly consented, and she went over for the wedding. Being an immortal with supernatural powers she punished him very severely during the wedding night and he promised to repent and never do such a thing again. Then Chang Ch'i-chieh returned to Ts'ui Wên-jui. Wên-jui, on account of the large bride-price he received, became well-to-do. Chang Ch'i-chieh stayed with him for several years and bore him a son. Then she left him and returned to heaven. She had fulfilled the curse, punished the wicked, and rewarded a filial son. ①

This popular version of the origin myth of Yü Huang is entertaining, moral, and exegetical. There may be anachronisms and false explanations in the story but it is certainly a masterpiece of Chinese folk literature. Popular tales without documentary evidence are always very difficult to date. This

---

① The legend is often dramatized on the rural stage in Centra and West China. During the late fall when the paddy harvest is in and the nights still warm, an open air stage is erected, and the play given.

story is based on the *Fêng shên Chuan* which was probably composed about the period A.D. 1567-1620 by an anonymous author.[1] There is no way of knowing how much older the story may be. Many of the legends contained in the *Fêng Shên, Chuan* are of considerable antiquity, and this compilation may only represent a phase of literary documentation and standardization. Even during the time of Ssŭ-ma Ch'ien, Chiang T'ai-kung was often connected with the supernatural. In the *Fêng Shan Shu* of the *Shih Chi* (ch. 28), it is said that "The eight divine generals existed from antiquity; some say that they were instituted from the time of T'ai-kung."[2] The apotheosis of Chiang T'ai-kung may have occurred quite early and culminated in the *Fêng Shên Chuan*. But how and when the origin myth of Yü Huang was grafted to him cannot be definitely determined at the present. To judge from the distribution of the window sill cult of Chiang T'ai-kung, which is almost universal in China, it may be of considerable antiquity.

[原载 *Harvard Journal of Asiatic Studies,* Vol. I,

No.2(1936),pp.242−250]

---

[1] 鲁迅:中国小说史略, 187-191. The *Fêng shên Chuan* was mentioned by Chang Wu-chiu 张无咎 in his preface to the *P'ing Yao Chuan* 平妖传, composed in the year 1620. Thus, the date of composition of the *Fêng shên Chuan* cannot be later than this.

[2] 史记, 封禅书."八神将自古而有之;或曰,太公以来作之."E. CHAVANNES, *Les Mémoires historiques de Se-ma Ts'ien* (3. 432) translates this passage as: "Les huit dieux ont existe dès l'antiquite². D'autres disent que c'està partir de l'Auguste duc qu'on fit (les sacrifices aux huit dieux)." In note 2 of the same page, he says: "Dans l'expression 将自古, le mot 将 a le sens de ' immédiatement, aussitôt.'·Chavannes' interpretation of the word 将 is rather arbitrary, so he has to omit it in his translation because it does not make sense in French. Such an interpretation, however, does not make sense in Chinese either!

TEKNONYMY AS A FORMATIVE FACTOR IN THE CHINESE KINSHIP SYSTEM[①]

The Chinese kinship system[②] is primarily built upon the foundation of the old patronymic sib organization[③] and the sharp differentiation of generations. All relatives, both lineal and collateral of the same patronym

---

① The author desires to express his deep gratitude to Prof A. I. Hallowell for his many painstaking corrections and criticisms.

② The earliest study of the Chinese relationship system was made by Lewis H. Morgan in his *Systems of Consanguinity and Affinity of the Human Family* (1870) which gave 196 terms. Subsequently G. Schlegel, A. G. May, G. Jamieson, P. G. von Möllendorff, and Pierre Hoang also dealt with the subject. The more recent and thorough studies are by H. P. Wilkinson, *Chinese Family Nomenclature and Its Supposed Relation to Primitive Group-marrige* (in *The Family in Classical China*, 1926, Chapter 13, pp. 157-210) and by T. S. Chen and J. K. Sbryock, Chinese Relationship Terms (*American Anthropologist*, Vol. 34, 1932, pp. 623-64). A. L. Kroeber made a very illuminating analysis of the Chinese system (based on Chen and Shryock's article) in his *Process in the Chinese Kinship System* (*American Anthropologist*, Vol. 35, 1933, pp. 151-57).

③ There is practically no literature on this important subject in English. For a very generalized conception, the reader may consult L. K. Tao, *Some Chinese Characteristics in the Light of the Chinese Family* (in *Essays Presented to C. G. Seligman*, 1934).

are classed into one "sib relation" group and all relatives by marriage, including women of the same patronym married out, are classed into the "outside relation" group. The generation principle cuts horizontally through these two groups of relatives and divides them into successive generation strata. These two factors—sib and generation—not only pervade the whole system, but also regulate marriage. A Chinese can marry any one outside his or her patronymic sib; if they are related they must be of the same generation irrespective of age. If the kinship system regulates marriage at all, it is only in the derivative sense.

Since generation is an important factor in the Chinese system, we should expect it to be consistently carried through. But there are some notable exceptions in contemporary usage, such as the fact that mother's brothers and wife's brothers are designated by the same term *chiu*, mother's sisters and wife's sisters by the same term *yi*, father's older brothers and husband's older brothers by the same term *po,* father's younger brothers and husband's younger brothers by the same term *shu*, father's sisters and husband's sisters by the same term *ku* (as hsiao ku).[1] These peculiarities are of significance because the Chinese system is not inherently an inconsistent one, but, as Morgan has remarked, it "embodies a well considered plan, which works out its results in a coherent and harmonious manner."[2] It is

---

[1] The Chinese characters are not given in this paper. Nearly all the terms used here can be found in the tables in Chen and Shryock's paper cited above, where the Chinese characters are given in full.

[2] L. H. Morgan, op. cit., p. 421.

still more significant, as we shall show later, that originally the generations of these relatives were clearly differentiated by distinct terms but in the course of time they gradually merged into each other. There must be at work some powerful disruptive force which threw the generation of these relatives into confusion.

There is one advantage in dealing with the Chinese kinship system: the terms are amenable to historical treatment. The changes of every term can be traced from period to period, and the causes of these changes can be, in most cases, ascertained. First we may take the connotations of the term *chiu* and the terms for the wife's brother during the various periods and arrange them in a table.[①]

Period	*Connotations of chiu*	*Terms for wife's brother*
I. Before 3rd century B.C.	mother's brother husband's father wife's father	sheng
II. 2nd century B.C. to 9th century A.D.	mother's brother	chi hsiung ti
III. 10th century A.D. to present	mother's brother wife's brother	chiu

The different connotations of the term *chiu* in Period I are perfectly intelligible in view of the fact that cross-cousin marriage was undoubtedly

---

①　The chief reference is Liang Chang-chü's *Ch'êng-wei-lu* (Book of Addresses) in which the first eight books are about kinship terms. This work is a laborious and comprehensive collection of terms from all periods.

in vogue at this time.① In such a marriage the mother's brother and husband's father would be the same person; so also would be mother's brother and wife's father. In Period II cross-cousin marriage was dropped, so correspondingly the meaning of *chiu* became confined to mother's brother.②

The terms for the wife's brother were different during each of the three periods. In Period I wife's brother was called *sheng. Sheng* also meant at this period father's sister's sons, mother's brother's sons, and sisters' husbands (man speaking). ③ This is also explicable by cross-cousin marriage of the bilateral type together perhaps with sister exchange. In Period Ⅱ, because of the disappearance of this type of marriage, *sheng* was no longer applicable to any of these relatives and new terms were introduced to take its place. *Chi hsiung ti*④ was the term used for wife's brothers.

In Period Ⅲ the term *chiu* (mother's brother) was extended to include wife's brothers. The first use of *chiu* in this new meaning is to be found in the *Hsin T'ang Shu*.⑤ In the Biography of Chu Yen-shou, it says: "Yang Hsing-mi's wife is the older sister of Chu Yen-shou. Hsing-mi (in ordering

---

① For cross-cousin marriage in ancient China, see Chen and Shryock, op.cit., p. 630.

② The new terms in the modern system for husband's father is kung and for wife's father yo fu.

③ Chen and Shryock, op. cit, pp. 630, 657.

④ It is purely a descriptive term. Chi means wife, hsiung ti means brothers, older and younger. Sometimes *fu hsiung* ti and *nei hsiung ti* were used. Both *fu* and *nei* mean wife. The new term for father's sister's sister's sons and mother's brother's sons is *piao hsiung ti*; *tzu fu* is the term for older sister's husband, and *mei fu* for younger sister's husband.

⑤ New Annals of the T'ang dynasty (A.D. 618-905), Book 189, p. 10 (Tung wên-edition of the Twenty-four Histories). In this article only the authentic reference of the first occurrence of a new term or the new use of an older term is given. The numerous later references are omitted for the sake of brevity.

Chu Yen shou to take up an important position) says: 'I am so sick and my sons are too young. Having *chiu* take my place, I shall have no worry'.'" This is certainly a curious extension of the use of *chiu*. Through all the vicissitudes of the term during the previous periods, the generation element was always preserved.[1] This blending of generations certainly warrants explanation.

In a strict sociological interpretation, the conclusion would be a mariage with the wife's brother's daughter as an extension of the sororate, [2]because in such a case the wife's brother would be a potential father-in-law. We see in Period I *chiu* also meant father in law. Since the wife's brother is a potential father in law, so the extension of the term *chiu* to him is perfectly logical. However there are several very serious difficulties to this interpretation. In the first place there is absolutely no evidence, either historical or contemporary, to support this hypothesis. In the second place it is contrary to the generation principle. Wife's brother's daughter will be one generation lower than ego; so in the Chinese system she is within the incest group. The third is a temporal difficulty. *Chiu* ceased to mean wife's

---

[1]　Indeed the Chinese system does not allow such complete departure from the generation principle, for in modern colloquial usage, special modifiers are used to differentiate the generations: such as mother's brothers are called *chiu fu*; *fu* indicates they belong to the "father" generation. Wife's brothers are called *chiu hsiung* and *chiu ti*; *hsiung* and *ti* indicate they belong to the "brother" generation.

[2]　The question of the sororate during the feudal period was discussed in full by Marcel Granet in *La polygynie sororale et la sororate dans la Chine féodale* (1920). There are many exaggerations and twistings of evidence in this work; however, the discussion is very lively.

father at least a thousand years before it was extended to mean wife's brother. In the face of these objections this interpretation is not tenable.

It is significant that Chinese scholars had been employing teknonymy to explain this anomaly long before its introduction into ethnological discussion by E. B. Tylor.[1] Ch'ien Ta-hsin (1727-1804), one of the most exacting classical scholars of his time, attributed this extension of the meaning of *chiu* to the gradual and imperceptible effect of the practice of teknonymy.[2] Wife's brothers are *chiu* to one's own children. The father adopts the language of his children, so he also calls his wife's brothers *chiu*. This can be clearly seen from the instance of Chu Yen-shou. Yang Hsing mi called Chu Yen-shou *chiu* together with the mentioning of his own sons. It is inferable that after long teknonymous usage the term *chiu* established itself and displaced the older term.

Whether this hypothesis can be sustained or not depends upon the additional evidences which we can adduce for its support. At this point we may turn to the examination of the terms which the wife uses to address her husband's father's brothers and her husband's brothers. Curiously, a similar mixing of generations occurs.

Po means father's older brothers (both man and woman speaking)

---

[1]   *On a Method of Investigating the Development of Institutions, etc.*(*Journal, Royal Anthropological Institute*, Vol. 18, pp. 245-69, 1889).

[2]   *Hêng-yen-lu* (Books Ordinary Sayings), Chüan 3.

〔husband's father's older brothers (wife adopting husband's term)〕①

husband's older brothers

Shu means father's younger brothers (both man and woman speaking)

〔husband's father's younger brothers (wife adopting husband's term)〕

husband's younger brothers

So far as I am aware, there is no social or marital usage in China, nor is there any comparable usage that ethnolographic data suggest, which could produce such a terminology. From the historical point of view, the terms for these relations were different at different periods. In the *Erh Ya,* ② the father's older brothers were called *shih fu.*③ From the second century B.C. to the third century A.D. *po fu* was generally used. From the fourth century A.D. and onward only *po* was sometimes used. Husband's older brothers were called *hsiung kung* in the *Erh Ya.*④ During the succeeding centuries, *hsiung chang* was commonly employed. About the tenth century

---

① A man or woman calls his or her father's older brothers *po* and father's younger brothers *shu*. The category of the sex of the speaker is usually not distinguished by terms in most cases in the Chinese system. When a woman marries, she adopts her husband's terms in addressing her father-in-law's brothers, e.g., as *po* and *shu*. There is no special term used by the wife for her father-in-law's brothers. See Chen and Shryock, op. cit., p. 640.

② The *Erh Ya* is the earliest Chinese dictionary; variously attributed to Chou Kung (B.C.?-1105) and to the disciples of Confucius (B.C. 551-479). Probably it is not a work by one hand but gradually augmented through many centuries. Its date cannot be much later than the fifth century B.C. The section on relationship terms has been translated by Chen and Shryock, op.cit, pp. 654-60.

③ *Erh Ya*, Chen and Shryock translation, p. 655. Both man and woman speaking, wife's term for them being the same.

④ Ibid., p. 659.

A.D., *po* was extended to mean husband's older brothers.[1] As has been already stated, no possible explanations can be found in marriage forms for this blending of generations: the only possible alternative is teknonymy. Husband's older brothers will be *po* to the wife's own children. The mother adopts the terminology of her children, so she also calls them *po*. The term *shu* can be similarly explained.

Ku in the modern system means:

father's sisters (both man and woman speaking)

〔husband's father's sisters (wife adopting husband's term)〕

husband's sisters

In Period I *ku* was used to mean father's sisters, husband's mother, and wife's mother (as *wai ku*) due to cross-cousin marriage.[2] When cross-cousin marriage declined, *ku* was employed only for father's sisters.[3] Husband's older sisters were called *nü kung* in the *Erh Ya* .[4] *Nü shu* or *shu mei* were also used a little later for the younger sisters of the husband. During the fourth century A.D., the term *ku* began to be extended to husband's sisters.[5] What was the cause of this extension cannot be exactly ascertained although

---

[1] *Ch'êng-wei-lu*, Chüan 7, p. 6. Most of the chronologies in this paper are based on this work.

[2] Chen and Shryock, op. cit., p. 630.

[3] The modern term for husband's mother is P'o or P'o P'o, literally "old lady". The term for wife's mother is *yo mu*.

[4] *Erh Ya,* op.cit., p. 659.

[5] The first occurrence of *hsiao ku* (husband's younger sisters) is in the famous poem *Kung chiao lung nan fei*. The exact date of this poem is disputed but all scholars agree it cannot be later than the fourth century A.D. *Ta ku* is used for husband's older sisters. *Ta* means big, senior; *hsiao* means small, junior.

the social history of the period concerned is fairly well known. It cannot be due to marriage with the wife's brother's daughter, in which case the husband's sister would be elevated to the position of the husband's father's sister: the objections to the interpretation of chín by this usage also apply here. Furthermore, other features do not follow either terminologically [1] or conceptually[2]. Teknonymy remains the best explanation, because husband's sisters will be *ku* of the wife's children.

Correspondingly we find the same peculiarity of blending of generations of mother's sisters with wife's sisters. Both are called *yi*. Originally *yi* was used, as in the *Erh Ya*,[3] for wife's sisters. Mother's sisters were called *tsung mu*.[4] The first use of *yi* to mean mother's sisters is found in the *Tso Chüan*. In the twenty-third year (B.C. 550) of Duke Hsiang there is a passage: "Yi's daughter of Mu-chiang." [5] By checking the marriages among the feudal lords of this time, it is clear that the term *yi* here does not mean wife's sister,

---

[1]　As among the Miwok where marriage with the wife's brother's daughter is reflected by twelve terms (E. W. Gifford, *Miwok Moieties*, University of California Publications in American Archaeology and Ethnology, Vol. 12, 1916, p. 186), but they are all lacking in the Chinese system.

[2]　Among the Omaha marriage with the wife's brother's daughter is reflected by the conceptual identification of the father's sister, the female ego, and the brother's daughter (A.Lesser, *Kinship Origins in the Light of Some Distributions*, *American Anthropologist*, Vol.31, 1929, pp. 711-12) although not indicated by the terminology. In the Chinese system the generations of the father's sisters, husband's father's sister, and the husband's sisters are clearly distinguished conceptually although the terminology fails to differentiate them.

[3]　*Erh Ya*, op. cit., p. 657.

[4]　Ibid., p. 656.

[5]　James Legge (*The Chinese Classics*, etc., Vol. 5, Part 2, p. 503) translated this passage: "A daughter of the younger sister of Muh-Këang (the mother of duke Ch'ing) .... " This is certainly a mistranslation. Legge not only did not check up the marriages among the feudal lords, but he did not even read the commentaries carefully.

as it ought, but mother's sister. As a matter of fact it ought to say *"tsung mu's* daughter of *Mu-chiang"* not *"yi's* daughter." This passage has perplexed the classical commentators for centuries and it still baffles the modern social anthropologist. Theoretically, a sororate together with a marriage with the father's widows would adequately explain it. In such a marriage, mother's sisters would be equated with wife's sisters. This explanation has certain plausibility, as a man's secondary wives are also called *yi*. That is mother's sisters, wife's sisters, and secondary wives (concubines) are all grouped into one class; a usage usually attributed to the sororate. It is well known that the sororate was practiced among the feudal lords, but as to the inheriting of father's widows there is no evidence. Indeed, such a marriage would be abhorrent to the ancient Chinese. We learn from the old writers how they compared the Hsiung-nu, pastoral nomads of the northern steppes, to dogs as they married their father's widows.

The consensus of opinion among the classical commentators about the discarding of *tsung mu* and the extension of *yi* to mean mother's sister is the psychological similarity between these relatives. Mother's sisters are *yi* to one's father just as wife's sisters are *yi* to oneself. The son imitates the language of his father, so he calls his father's *yi* also *yi*. In short this case seems to demand a psychological explanation [1] together with a reverse

---

[1] A. L. Kroeber, *Classificatory Systems of Relationship* (*Journal, Royal Anthropological Institute*, Vol. 39, 1909, pp. 77-84). Kroeber's views on liuguo-psychological causation of kinship nomenclature have been much attacked by students. For an equitable comment see A. Lesser, op. cit., p. 711.

teknonymy.

The foregoing cases are the only instances in the Chinese system where the generation principle is openly violated. In every case we have tried to explain these exceptions by facts and hypotheses which have proved illuminating in the discussion of analogous phenomena elsewhere. But we found none of them applicable to the Chinese material. Instead, we found teknonymy the only satisfactory explanation. There is no doubt that teknonymy is the determining factor in all these cases, but we may ask, is teknonymy universal in China and of sufficient antiquity that it may have been involved in producing such effects in the kinship terminology? There is no question about the universality of the practice in China; only the frequency of its use might have varied from time to time and from place to place. It is usually of the type that omits the child's name, just as in America, a man may call his wife simply "mother".

As to its antiquity, we have to depend upon historical evidence. Skipping the numerous comparatively late references, the earliest instance that can be interpreted as teknonymy is recorded in Kung yang's *Commentary of the Spring and Autumn Annals of Confucius*. In the sixth year (B.C. 489) of Duke Ai is recorded the instance of Ch'ên Ch'i. Ch'ên Chi in referring to his wife says "Mother of Ch'ang....". Ch'ang was known to be Ch'ên Ch'i's son. The teknonymous usage here is indubitably clear. The fifth century B.C. is more than a millenium earlier than most of the cases we have just discussed, except the case of *yi* (B.C. 550), which is more than half a century anterior. On the other hand, if we make allowance for the conservative spirit of the classical writers in recording colloquial language, it is reasonable to infer that teknonymy is much older than this documentary evidence shows.

In the very limited literature on teknonymy, various theories have been put forth to account for its origin, [1] but no author attempts to use it to explain other social phenomena. Teknonymy as a usage is based on kinship and kinship nomenclature—a circumlocutory way of expressing embarrassing relationships. Through its long and intensive use, why should it not have produced certain peculiarities in kinship terminologies as other social usages are reputed to have done? The Chinese cases are especially illuminating. It would require a series of marital or other special practices to explain the peculiarities of *chiu*, *po*, *shu*, *ku*, and *yi*, whereas they can be uniformly explained by a single principle—teknonymy.

[原载 *American Anthropologist*, Vol.38, No.1(1936), pp.59-66]

---

[1]　R.H. Lowie, *Primitive Society* (New York, 1920), pp. 107-109, 262.